LIFE OF
"BIG FOOT" WALLACE

W. A. A. "Big Foot" Wallace

LIFE OF
"BIG FOOT" WALLACE
The Great Ranger Captain

❖

by

A. J. Sowell

❖

Introduction by

Mike Cox

Illustrated by Charles Shaw

❖

STATE HOUSE PRESS
Austin, Texas
1989

Rare
F
390
.W26
S69
1989

Copyright ©1989 State House Press (new material)
Originally published in 1899
All Rights Reserved

Library of Congress Cataloging-in-Publication Data

Sowell, A. J. (Andrew Jackson), 1848-1921.
Life of "Big Foot" Wallace : the great Ranger captain / by A.J. Sowell ; new introduction by Mike Cox ; illustrated by Charles Shaw.
p. cm.
Includes index.
ISBN 0-938349-35-X : $19.95. — ISBN 0-938349-36-8 (pbk.) : $12.95. — ISBN 0-938349-37-6 (deluxe lim.) : $50.00
1. Wallace, Big-Foot, 1817-1899. 2. Pioneers—Texas—Biography. 3. Frontier and pioneer life—Texas. 4. Texas Rangers—Biography. 5. Texas—History—Republic, 1836-1946. 6. Texas—History—1846-1950. I. Title.
F390.W26S69 1989
976.4'04'0924—dc19 89-4246
[B] CIP

Manufactured in the United States of America

Frontispiece photograph and Appendix letter courtesy of Gianfranco Spellman, D.V.M.

State House Press
P.O. Box 15247
Austin, Texas 78761

CONTENTS

CONTENTS

INTRODUCTION

W. A. A. "Big Foot" Wallace was an unusual man, and so was the author of this biography, Andrew Jackson Sowell. Like Wallace, Sowell had ridden with the Texas Rangers. Hundreds of men could have made that claim, but Sowell did something that few of his colleagues ever bothered to do—he wrote about his experiences, and about other Rangers and early-day Texans. Sowell not only was a fair hand at Indian fighting, he was a good writer.

Born August 2, 1848 near Seguin in Guadalupe County, Andrew Jackson Sowell in a way was already a third-generation Texan, though he was the first generation of his family born in Texas. His grandfather, John Sowell, came to Texas with DeWitt's colonists in 1829 and aided in Texas' fight for independence by making and repairing guns. He also made a wide-bladed knife for James Bowie, a distinctive weapon that would bear Bowie's name. Sowell's father, Asa J. L. Sowell, was too young to fight in the Revolution, but later served with Capt. Jack Hays' Texas Rangers and was a pioneer Guadalupe County settler.

The younger Sowell joined the Rangers on Nov. 5, 1870 and served in Company F of the Frontier Battalion under Capt. David P. Baker. He participated in the Wichita Campaign in Northwest Texas. As he would write in his first book, *Rangers and Pioneers of Texas* (1884), he "experienced some very hard service" as a Ranger. Sowell and his fellow Rangers endured a harsh winter and took part in several Indian fights.

Records in the State archives show that Sowell served through June 15, 1871. When he was mustered out, he was due $325 in pay, less $135 for one horse, $50 for another horse, $30 for a Winchester carbine, $10 for a McClellan saddle, $12 for an overcoat, $3.50 for a blanket and $58.00 for "goods." Sowell may not have made much money risking his scalp for the people of Texas, but he was amply compensated in thrilling experiences.

Big Foot Wallace was a legendary Texas figure long before Sowell decided to do a book on the old Ranger. The year Sowell left the Rangers, John D. Duval published his *Adventures of Big Foot Wallace.* Duval, who had served with Wallace as a Ranger, had a colorful way with words, but Wallace did not like the book. Wallace apparently was interested in setting the record straight, which probably explains why the grizzled frontiersman was agreeable to working with Sowell. And Wallace, who had served under Hays, surely knew Sowell's father.

Sowell produced his biography of Wallace just in time. The Ranger's long life was near its end. When the book was written, Wallace, then 81, was living in Frio County with W. W. "Doc" Cochran and his family. Their place was three miles from the small community of Big Foot, which had been named in the Ranger's honor, and five miles from Devine.

As Sowell explained in his 1900 book, *Early Settlers and Indian Fighters of Southwest Texas,* he had spent several weeks with Wallace while the Ranger was staying with Cochran. "I never tired of listening to him talk," Sowell wrote.

This stay with Wallace was evidently when Sowell did his interviewing for the biography. While in Frio County, Sowell must have made an arrangement with *The Devine News,* which printed the first edition of the book.

In October 1898, Wallace got word to Sowell that if Sowell would come get him, he would like to go to a Ranger reunion at the State Fair in Dallas. Sowell must have jumped at the chance to spend more time with the famous Ranger. "Accordingly I did so," he wrote, "and we had a fine time. Big Foot Wallace was as great a show as anything else on the (fair) grounds. All had heard of him, and wanted to talk to him and take him by the hand."

On October 20, Sowell returned to Frio County with Wallace. It was the last time he would see the old frontiersman. Just after Christmas, Wallace became seriously ill, possibly with pneumonia. He died on January 7, 1899 and was buried in the Devine Cemetery, in Medina County. A short time after Wallace's death, the Legislature convened and a bill was passed authorizing Wallace's burial in the State Cemetery in Austin. His body was exhumed and reburied in Austin. The gravestone bears this short epitaph:

BIG FOOT WALLACE
Here Lies He Who Spent His
Manhood Defending the Homes
of Texas
Brave Honest and Faithful
Born April 3, 1817
Died Jan. 7, 1899

The publication date of Sowell's book is shown as 1899. From the content, it is obvious the manuscript had been completed while Wallace was still alive. Whether the printing was completed before Wallace's death, or just after, is not known. Whatever the circumstances, Sowell waited until 1900, when his next book was published to complete Wallace's story in a 36-page sketch.

Andrew Jackson Sowell would live for another generation. Sowell went on to write *A History of Fort Bend County* in 1904 and *Incidents Connected with the Early History of Guadalupe County, Texas* (n.d.). In addition to his books, Sowell wrote feature articles for the *San Antonio Express* and other publications. Nearing his 70th birthday, Sowell wrote a story for the *Express* on the Big Bend, the last semblance of wild country in Texas. Sowell said in the 1918 article that he had been in the Trans-Pecos for three years, camping with his son Lee, who was being paid by ranchers to hunt and trap mountain lions. There is some indication Sowell was working on another book at the time of his death in the Kerr County community of Center Point in 1921, but the manuscript apparently has not survived.

Both Wallace and Sowell have some notable company in their respective final resting places. The graves of 32 former Rangers, including Sowell's, have been identified in the Center Point Cemetery. The cemetery is believed to have more Ranger burials than any other graveyard in Texas.

Sowell's biography of Wallace was long out of print by the time of Sowell's death. In 1927, J. Marvin Hunter, who had known both Sowell and Wallace, reprinted *The Life of Big Foot Wallace* in several installments of his magazine *Frontier Times.* He later issued the book in pamphlet form. In 1938, an edition of 500 was brought out. The book sold for $1 a copy, the proceeds earmarked for an addition to Hunter's Frontier Times Museum in Bandera.

Sowell's book eventually went out of print again and remained difficult to find until 1957, when the Steck Co. of Austin brought out a facsimile edition of the original *Devine News* printing. This hardback volume, with added color illustrations by Ralph White and photographs of Wallace from the collection of Ed Bartholomew, was distributed by the printing company as a Christmas gift and is also long out of print.

For this new edition, the publishers have reset Sowell's text, provided new illustrations and prepared the first-ever index of the book. Some lengthy sentences have been broken up and a few instances of language that today would be considered racially offensive have been changed. Otherwise, the content is the same as it was in 1899, when the frontier was still fresh on the minds of living men.

Without question, Big Foot Wallace was one of Texas' most colorful frontier characters. He, and other Rangers, helped make early day Texas a safer place to live. Andrew Jackson Sowell not only did his share of rangering, but as an author left for all of us a record of how it was done.

Mike Cox
February, 1989

PREFACE

At all times during the past ages, ever since man began to have a history, it has been a custom among men for some one to keep a record of noted events and of individuals; men who have stepped aside from the ordinary walks of life, and have made themselves a name as statesmen, warriors, generals and frontiersmen, and in many other ways. America has been the widest field for men to achieve fame as scouts, trailers and Indian fighters from the time of Miles Standish and Captain Church almost to the present time. In this list of noted frontiersmen, we find the names of many who have a national reputation, such as Daniel Boone, Benjamin Logan, Simon Kenton, Buffalo Bill, Wild Bill, Edward Burleson, Jack Hays and Big Foot Wallace.

The time has now passed in the United States for men to achieve fame as Indian fighters, but let us keep the memory green of those who stood between civilization and the red path of the savage. They cut the brush and blazed the way for others to follow. They subdued the wild beast, and wilder men, but they are fast dropping aside from the walks of men, and soon none will be left to tell the tale of frontier days. Now is the time while a few of them are left, to get correct history.

The facts contained in this book were gathered by the writer from the old frontiersman himself. He says that other works purporting to be his history are not true; not even the origin of his name. One of the objects of this book is to give the people a true history of the many stirring events in the life of the great Ranger Captain. The name of Big Foot Wallace in after years will be to Texas what Daniel Boone's was to Kentucky.

A. J. SOWELL

CHAPTER I

ANCESTORS

William Alexander Anderson Wallace, better known as "Big Foot," was born in Lexington, Rockbridge County, Virginia, on the 3d day of April, at 5 o'clock in the morning in the year 1817. He weighed 13 lbs, and his nurse said he could kick harder and yell louder than any youngster she ever saw. Big Foot Wallace is of Celtic origin. His ancestors back to a very remote period lived in the Highlands of Scotland and his great-grandfather, Samuel Wallace, died there. They can trace themselves back to a near kinship to the famous Sir William Wallace, regent of Scotland and leader of the Scottish army in the war against King Edward of England. Also to Robert Bruce, through his grandmother Elizabeth Bruce. The Wallaces were all powerful men physically. The subject of this sketch in his prime was six feet two inches in his moccasins and weighed 240 lbs. He has long arms and large hands, and his hair before it turned grey was black and very thick and inclined to curl. He had one uncle who was seven feet in height, and one brother who was six feet and five inches. History states that Sir William Wallace was almost a giant in strength and none could stand before him in battle. The sword which he used in the war with Edward is preserved at Edinburgh and is a wonder to all that behold it on account of its size. It is also related that on one occasion as a historian was traveling in the Scottish Highlands gathering data, he learned that a very aged lady living near by had seen Sir William Wallace when she was a very small girl, but had a great memory and could tell many interesting incidents connected with the days of Bruce and Wallace. This author was anxious to get facts in regards to the great strength of Wallace and at once set out and found the ancient dame and made known his mission. "Oh yes" she says "I knew Sir William well, and also Sir Robert (Bruce). Sir Robert was a powerful man, he could" —here the gentleman interrupted her and said "but my good woman it was not of Bruce I asked, but of Wallace," "That's what I am telling you" she resumed, "As I was going to say Sir Robert was a fine man and Oh! what strength he had he—" "You are off again my dear madam. I am not writing the life of Robert Bruce but of Sir William Wallace and it is of him I wish you to speak." "Why man can't ye let me tell ye. I can never get to the point if ye put me out so much." The man now told her to go on and he would not bother her any more, so she resumed. "As I said before I knew Sir William and Sir Robert well. Sir Robert was a fine man and his strength was such that he could overthrow two common men but Sir William could overthrow two such as Sir Robert." She was going at it in this roundabout way so as to more forcibly illustrate the great strength of Wallace.

Samuel Wallace, grandfather of Big Foot, came to America after the death of his father whose name also was Samuel, as above stated. He settled in Virginia where the town of Lexington now is and at one time owned half of the land now covered by the city. This was prior to the revolutionary war. When it broke out, his grandfather and his grand uncles, William, James and Adam joined the American army. All of them, except the grandfather Samuel, lost their lives before the war was over. William came home on furlough and died one mile from Lexington. His body was the first one placed in the cemetery there and the longest one ever put there. He was seven feet in height. His death was likely caused from the terrible winter through which Washington's army passed without sufficient quarters when many died with maladies caused from cold.

Both the others were officers and men of great strength and both were killed in the battle of Guilford Court House in South Carolina. James was a colonel and Adam major. The command to which they belonged was cut off and massacred by Tarleton's cavalry; only one man named Plunket making his escape, and he did so by feigning death. This notorious cavalry and the "Queen's Rangers" commanded by Simcoe had the reputation of giving no quarter. They were the same fellows who massacred the small force at the Waxhaw settlement when Andrew Jackson, then a youth, was captured and who was wounded by an officer with a sabre because the young patriot would not black his boots. Many cavalry however, bit the dust at Guilford when the two Wallace brothers fell. To prove with what desperation these two fought, one has only to look at the swords which they used on that day and which are preserved by some members of the family at Lexington. Both are hacked and gapped from the hilt to the point. No common man could handle the one carried by James. It is six feet in length and heavy in proportion. The other is shorter but thick and heavy. It will be remembered by readers of American history that the American forces were defeated at Guilford and during their retreat, the British cavalry closely pressed the patriots and many were slain. It was here that Col. Wallace, rallying a portion of his men to cover the retreat, was cut off and hacked to pieces by Tarleton.

CHAPTER II

BROTHERS AND SISTERS - ON THE WAY TO TEXAS - HAD A FIGHT IN NEW ORLEANS - ARRIVES IN GALVESTON.

The father of Big Foot Wallace was named Andrew and his mother was Jane Ann Blair. There were six brothers of them named as follows according to age: James, Samuel, William A. A. (Big Foot), Joseph Blair, Andrew and Alexander Anderson. The latter it will be noticed had the middle name of Big Foot. There were three sisters: Rebecca Jane, Elizabeth, Martha, and one half-sister, Sarah Wallace. Rebecca married Marion Seahorn who died in California. Elizabeth died when she was fifteen years of age and Martha also died when young. Sarah Wallace married Charles Varner.

The subject of our sketch grew up on his father's farm near Lexington. They had a large orchard of very fine fruit and many people came there in the fruit season to get it. There was also many strawberries on the old Wallace farm. In this way, diversifying the time in farming, hunting and going to school, he spent the first twenty years of his life. He was fond of a gun and being alone in the woods. He would sometimes play truant from school and spend the day in his favorite pastime of hunting or fishing.

So that our readers who are not familiar with Texas history can better understand the times just preceding the advent of Big Foot into Texas, although he did not wear that name at the time, we will state that the Mexican government had held out extraordinary inducements to the people of the United States to settle in Texas. At that time in the early 1820's, Texas was a vast unsettled wilderness except for here and there an old Spanish mission around which clustered a few settlers. Over this vast domain of Texas, which was one thousand miles in length and six hundred in breadth, roamed twenty-two tribes of Indians. The country was the most beautiful almost of earth. Its warm climate, clear streams, vast herds of wild game and nutritious grasses made it a veritable paradise to look upon. Soon the restless American pioneers began to pour into it and up to the year 1835 many settlements had been made in the eastern and middle portions. However, by this time the Mexicans had become jealous and uneasy at the vast number that were coming in and therefore concluded to stop all further immigration of the Anglo Saxon race and disarm those who had already come. Santa Anna was now in power as president of Mexico and his brother-in-law General Cos was in command of a troop at San Antonio. In September of 1835 he sent a force to Gonzales in DeWitt's Colony to bring off a small cannon which had been furnished the Texans by the Mexicans for defense against the Indians. The settlers, believing that their rights were being encroached upon, refused to give it up and a fight ensued in which the Mexicans were defeated and returned to San Antonio. General Stephen F. Austin, who is called the father of Texas as he was the head of the immigration scheme, raised a force and marched upon San Antonio. Shortly after arriving there, two of his officers, Cols. James Bowie and Fannin, defeated a Mexican force sent out to meet them by Cos at the Mission Concepcion, below the city on the river. Several other skirmishes followed this battle, and then the town was stormed by Col. Ben Milam. Gen. Cos and his army were captured and then liberated and sent to

Mexico. There the defeated Cos, smarting under his discomfiture made known all these things to his august brother-in-law Santa Anna, president and dictator of Mexico.

When the news of the revolt of the Texans was heard in the States, many chivalrous and spirited young men at once flocked to Texas to aid their countrymen in their unequal struggle. Among these were Samuel Wallace, brother of Big Foot, and his cousin William Wallace. When Santa Anna heard of the victories of the Texans, he at once raised an army and led them in person in an invasion of Texas. In the meantime, most of the volunteers who had defeated the Mexicans at San Antonio, thinking their services were no longer needed, repaired to their homes and only a small force under W. B. Travis was left to garrison San Antonio. Col. Fannin with a somewhat larger force was sent to hold the post at Goliad.

This was the state of affairs when the invading army from Mexico arrived before San Antonio. The Texans retreated into the Alamo, and Col. Travis sent messengers to Fannin and to the people East, to the former asking him to come to his relief with his cannon and calling on the people of the Colonies to also raise men and come to him. Fannin attempted to come and bring his cannon, but his carts broke down so that he could not move his supplies or ordnance, so he went back with his men to Goliad.

The people in the East were aroused and in convention assembled at old Washington-on-the-Brazos, selected General Sam Houston to lead the armies of Texas to fight the invaders. While all this was going on, however, Santa Anna was besieging the Alamo and on the 6th day of March 1836, stormed the fort with six thousand men. All the Texans, numbering one hundred and eighty-four, perished to a man after fighting one of the most desperate battles ever recorded in history, except Leonidas and his three hundred Spartans at the pass of Thermopylae, but they had their messenger of defeat. The Alamo had none.

Santa Anna now sent a large force against Fannin, who, in trying to carry out the orders of General Houston, had evacuated the fort at Goliad and was overtaken by the Mexicans on the Coleto prairie. Here another desperate battle ensued which lasted all the evening and through the night. Many were killed and wounded and no water to be had. The cannon were rendered useless on account of having no water to cool them and when daylight came, Col. Fannin who had his leg broken in the battle and seeing no chance to break through the Mexican lines which now completely encompassed them, made terms with the Mexicans for a surrender. Nearly half of his men had been killed and wounded. The balance were still ready to fight, but at the request of their beloved and heroic commander, came forward and laid down their guns and pistols. Could they have foreseen the dreadful tragedy which was to ensue, they would have sprang forward and seizing them, once more drenched the plains of Coleto in blood. This, however, they could not foresee and allowed themselves to be disarmed and marched back to Goliad with a promise that in eight days they would be liberated. The way, however, that the Mexicans gave them liberty was to carry them out on the prairie when the eight days had expired, and shoot them down without any chance for their lives. Here Sam Wallace, brother of Big Foot and William Wallace, his cousin, lost their lives. They had joined the Georgia battalion and a braver set of young men never died for any country. Also here perished Major Benjamin Wallace, another relative whose people emigrated to Georgia and who came with the volunteers from that state. Besides these, there was one other Wallace killed there of the same connection making four of that historic name who with their blood watered the tree of Texas history.

News traveled slow in those days and it was a long time before the Wallace family learned from the newspapers of the day that the son and brother had met his death by treachery at the hands of the Mexicans. William Alexander (Big Foot) said he was going to Texas and avenge his brother and cousin's death. His father tried to dissuade him from the undertaking, but he was determined and said he would spend the balance of his days killing Mexicans. One thing that so exasperated him was the fact that his brother and cousin were put to death after they surrendered. He was young and strong of limb and handled his heavy rifle as an ordinary man would a cornstalk. As before stated he came of a family noted for their size and strength. His brother Andrew was six feet five inches in height and was killed in the seven days fight around Richmond during the civil war. Big Foot himself when in his prime on the frontiers of Texas was six feet two inches in his moccasins and weighed 240 lbs, had thick black curly hair and had a spread of arms of six feet and six inches.

Before Wallace could get off to Texas to take a hand in the struggle for liberty, news came of the famous battle of San Jacinto in which the Mexican army was overthrown and Santa Anna himself was taken which gave freedom to Texas and ended the war. Still he was bent on going and in the following year set out in company with his uncle, Joseph Blair, his cousin, James Paxton, and three other men named Reese, Gardiner and Warren. They came by way of New Orleans and remained a short time there. Big Foot, while circulating around town to see what was to be seen, unfortunately got into a difficulty with a man and knocked him through a fire screen into a fireplace. Seeing another of the party advancing on him with a heavy cane, he made a lunge at him with a knife, knocked off his lick and cut him severely with the knife in the side. In doing this he broke the rivet of the knife and put it in his pocket as he ran out and went to the hotel where his party was. They saw something was wrong, discovered blood on the pocket where he had replaced the bloody weapon and at once told him to throw the knife away and change pants after he had told them the circumstances. Search was made for him by officers but failed to locate him and in a few days their party began to look for a ship to carry them to Texas.

Wallace had a cousin in New Orleans named Samuel Ruff, who had been a surgeon in the United States Navy eight years, but had retired from that business. To him they went and he said he would show them a ship to take passage in as the Gulf was dangerous to cross and many ships were lost. The vessel he told them to take was the Diadem and said it was one of the best schooners afloat and would carry them through all right. So on the Diadem they took passage for Galveston, Texas. Little did the young Virginian dream of the fearful ordeals through which he would have to pass in the great West in Texas and in Mexico. A captive in the latter place, wearing chains, starved nearly to death, marched on foot from place to place, confined in the fearful dungeon of Perote, drawing beans for his life at Salado & etc., but we anticipate.

During the passage from New Orleans to Galveston their vessel encountered a fearful storm and it took a good ship indeed to weather it. As the saying is, waves rolled mountain high and the ship pitched and tossed something like a Texas bronco, only on a more colossal scale. All on the vessel got seasick except Wallace, sailors and all. They accused him of being a sailor when he would eat his regular meals when all the balance were so badly torn up and disgruntled in the region of the stomach. His uncle, a man of strong nerve, had to give in and as Wallace expressed it "puked like a dog and wished the whole damned thing would go to the bottom." There was but one woman aboard and she could not be still any where, but would tumble about all the time, out of a chair, out of her bunk or any place and would lay wherever she fell until Wallace (who was the only one who could do so) would pick her up and put her back where she fell from. He said he "wanted to keep her on her pegs if he could." When the ship arrived at Galveston, all on the ship except Wallace had to be carried ashore. This was the 5th day of October, 1837. Galveston had also suffered from the storm and all the shipping on the Gulf had been wrecked or driven ashore along the coast. Wallace says all that saved their party was the staunch ship his cousin had put them aboard at New Orleans.

Instead of going to bed as the balance did when they got ashore, Wallace went around to take a look at the place and soon saw two large schooners high and dry on some sand hills right in town. What was his surprise to see two men laying off a town, offering town lots for sale and tried to sell him one. "What!" he said, "make a town here where water was so deep a few days ago? I will take one however, if you will put mine on a boat." The man laughed and went on with his work.

CHAPTER III.

FIRST FIGHT WITH INDIANS, CAPTURED BY INDIANS

During the stay of Wallace and his party on the island of Galveston they visited the home and fort of the pirate Lafitte, where he lived when he was "monarch of all he surveyed, and his rights there was none to dispute" on the island. It was then, says Captain Wallace, at the time of their visit called Campeachy.

From Galveston the Virginians went to Bastrop on the Colorado, then an old settled place but few people there: Eglestone, Manlove and Mays. The latter having come from the same place Wallace did, and his people at home were not aware where he had drifted to.

The excitement of war being over in Texas, the uncle of Wallace concluded to go back to the old home, and tried to get him also to return. No, he said, this country just suited him, there was plenty of game and that was all he asked from any country, and here he was going to cast his fortunes, come what might. His cousin James Paxton also concluded to stay and went to Houston, then just starting, and got a position as clerk in a store, where he remained a year. He then decided to go back home, packed his trunk, went down to Harrisburg to take a boat for Galveston, and was seized with a malady something like choleramoribus while his trunk was being carried aboard, and in half an hour died and was buried at Harrisburg. The balance of the party, except Wallace, went back to Virginia.

From Bastrop Wallace drifted up to a settlement where LaGrange is now. Only one man lived there, Colonel John H. Moore, but eight others lived on the west side of the river opposite. Many people came on up the river hunting settlements and on one occasion while the Colorado was overflowed, quite a lot of immigrants were waterbound on the side which Col. Moore lived. He made a proposition that if they would stop there and settle he would lay off a town and they could get timber off his land to build houses. This was agreed to, the town was laid off and that is the way LaGrange started. Captain Wallace says that a man named Boone put up a saloon and one cold winter his whiskey froze and the people were under the impression that he watered it pretty freely.

The men who belonged to the Texas army during the war for independence were entitled to a grant of land, and so as to secure the land to which his brother Sam was entitled, Big Foot went to Houston and took out administration papers and administered on the estate after complying with all the laws relative to that kind of transaction. It was while here in Houston attending to that business that he first met General Sam Houston who went on his bond as administrator. A man from Georgia also signed the bond. The validity of the claim was proved up as to the identity of Sam Wallace by men who participated in the fearful battle, but made their escape during the butchery of the prisoners. These were Hunter, Neily and Smith, the two latter belonging to the same company as that of the unfortunate and gallant soldier.

Having attended to his business, Wallace went back to LaGrange and enjoyed the new country to his heart's content, hunting, going on scouts after hostile Indians and farming some. He rented land from Ed Manton, but almost failed, he says, of making a crop on account of going on so many scouts. His first fight with Indians was in 1838 when a band came down from the mountains and carried off stock in the vicinity of LaGrange, and then went on down the country. Big Foot Wallace and five other men struck the trail and followed after them. One of these men was Gorman Woods and another was named Black. Young Wallace was eager to have a battle and strained his eye to catch a sight of the hostiles as mile after mile was passed over on the trail. Finally they came into view, fifteen in number, traveling down the Colorado valley below Bastrop. Some of the men were Indian fighters, especially Black, and the men were told to gallop toward them and scatter some as they went and if the Indians made a stand to fight, to dismount and shoot so their aim would be better, but if they ran, for each man to single out an Indian and pursue him, running on his right forty or fifty yards away so the Indian could not effectually use his bow without turning. When the Indians discovered that they were pursued they scattered and commenced a precipitate flight. The chase lasted several miles, each man urging his horse, trying to come within shooting distance of an Indian. Occasionally the crack of a rifle was heard and when the chase was over two Indians were dead and one wounded. Wallace succeeded in getting up to within fifty yards of one and getting in a good shot that brought him from his horse dead. The Indians used bows and shot wild in the flight and did not succeed in hurting anyone. At this time there were immigrants moving near where the fight took place or at least on a line of their flight. The Indians came upon them and sent one of their number covered with a bear skin to spy them out. While the party was at supper a negro servant who was out looking around came in and said he saw a bear. His master told him to take a gun and shoot it. The negro did so and wounded the Indian, but he got away. When Wallace and his party arrived and found the Indians has passed there, they took up the trail next day and found the Indian who still had on the bear skin and had been left by his companions. The man Black got down and shot him again and then scalped him before he died. Wallace says this was a new and horrible sight to him, especially as the Indian tried to turn and look the white man in the face while his scalp was being taken off. Black was a regular Indian hunter and showed them no quarter. The Indians had killed all of his family. Black also took part of the skin from the Indian's body and made razor strops out of it.

On one occasion Wallace went down to San Felipe and there met up with Judge R. M. Williamson "Three Legged Willie" who said to him "Hello young man, what brought you to Texas?" Young Wallace replied, "I had more wives than the law allowed me and could think of no better place to come than Texas." The Judge laughed at this and asked him to come in and take a drink with him, which he politely declined to do. Another man in the crowd walked up and said he would make him drink. Wallace now faced the man and said "My Friend, you will have to spell able first." At this juncture Judge Williamson drew a pistol and said to the aggressive man: "Let that young fellow alone. If he does not want to drink today, sometime likely we will meet in the road and he will have a full bottle and we will want a drink." Wallace stayed five years in Texas before taking a drink of whiskey or a cup of coffee.

The country along the Colorado being new and sparsely settled, game was in abundance, and Wallace being fond of hunting and being alone in the woods, took long trips on foot with his rifle on his shoulder looking at the country and shooting game as desired. On one of these occasions he was captured by the Indians. He had gone to Buckners Creek especially to kill a deer and was surprised to find none in this noted range when he arrived there. They were generally in droves and no trouble to kill. Search where he would now, none could be found. The cause of this absence of the deer was the fact that Indians were around and they had been scared off. The disappointed hunter walked about until he became tired and then sat down on a post oak log to rest. In a short time, however, he was surprised and somewhat alarmed to see an Indian suddenly step in front of him and stop. Wallace sprang to his feet in an instant and aimed his gun at him but was at once surrounded by a large body of Indians, all aiming their arrows at him, and making signs for him to lay down his gun. Wallace now thinking that he had no chance for his life, backed against a tree and determined to sell it as dearly as possible, still aimed his gun at them and they still drew their arrows as if to shoot. The first Indian who had come in front of Wallace while he was sitting on the log and who was the chief, now motioned for all of the Indians to leave, which they did at once and soon disappeared in the thickets near by. The chief then turned and walked off, beckoning for the white man to follow him. Feeling relieved that he was not executed at once and knowing that a hundred snaky eyes were watching from cover close by and would send fifty arrows into his body in case harm befell their chief, Wallace at once quit his tree and followed. The chief led the way through the thickets and tangled forest until he came to a large Indian encampment. A curious crowd of squaws, children, old men and young bucks gathered around him and he was told to sit down on the ground. Soon the warriors who had been left behind silently came in and a council was held among them. One made a speech and when he was through, another got up and so on. While this was going on Wallace had time for reflection. Only a short time before he was at home in Lexington, Virginia, and his parents trying to persuade him to abandon his trip and run the risk of losing his own life in Texas trying to avenge the death of his brother. But his Celtic blood was up and go he would, but now he was a captive among the Indians in the wilds of Texas, and his captors were then, no doubt, debating whether they should put him to death or not. A squaw soon came out of a wigwam and she also made a talk. Taking Wallace by the hand, she led him into the wigwam, showed him some meat, and made signs for him to sit down, cook and eat. He was satisfied now that he was safe for the present, but determined to escape at the first opportunity. In two weeks he seemed to like his new life well, as they allowed him to go out on a hunt with the chief's son. Wallace soon left him and went back to the settlement; but what was his surprise when he arrived to find the chief had preceded him, and wanted to make a treaty with the whites. The chief's son had hastily returned when Wallace had walked off from him and told the news of his escape. The chief fearing the anger of the whites, took a near cut, and being fleet of foot, arrived first. The Indians had been pretending to be friendly. The people had been very uneasy about Wallace, and looked for him and buzzard signs, far and near, and thought he had been killed.

The chief now set out in company with some white men, including Wallace, and went to see General Houston and make a treaty with him. The chief was afraid some of the white men might shoot him, so he put part of his blanket around Wallace, and they went in that way together. Houston, who was always a friend to the Indians, made a treaty with the chief, who was greatly pleased and said Houston was the smartest man he ever saw, and himself the next.

These were Lipan Indians who made treaties and broke them at will. They were a branch of the Apaches and always treacherous.

CHAPTER IV

FIRST TRIP TO SAN ANTONIO.
VIEWING THE RUINS OF THE ALAMO.

On the 14th day of April 1838, a fine muscular looking young man might have been seen standing among the ruins of the Alamo in San Antonio, gazing upon the scene of the desperate battle which took place there two years before, when the gallant Travis and his heroes put themselves in front of the advancing host of invaders. It was only over their dead bodies that Santa Anna could hurl his legions against the settlers in the east. The young man in question, who stood there with flashing eye and surveyed the scene of the fierce struggle, was Big Foot Wallace, then unknown to fame and who had just arrived from the Colorado. For the first time he had tread the streets of San Antonio and gazed upon the sacred spot around the dismantled fort of the Alamo. The signs of the battle were on every side. An outer wall enclosed the Alamo in front and reached out into the plaza, where there was an entrance through two large gates. The walls had been partly demolished by cannon shots, and the gates had been torn and twisted around. Piles of rock were here and there scattered promiscuously about. The ashes were still to be seen where the slain Texans were burned and Wallace turned up small pieces of charred bones while raking about among them. All the larger pieces of bones had been collected and buried and only small bits remained that had been overlooked. The first Mexicans Wallace saw after coming to

Texas were Rodriguez and Manchaca, down near Houston, who were carrying a dispatch from General Rusk to General Houston. They could talk English and Wallace stopped and conversed with them awhile.

They had Spanish gourds to carry water in, and they were a curiosity to the newly arrived Virginian.

There were no canteens in those days and these gourds took their place. They were peculiarly adapted to carrying water. They were of various sizes holding from a pint to two gallons and were very small in the middle, not more than two inches or less in diameter and large at each end with a small neck for a mouth piece. A strong piece of rawhide or buckskin was tied around the small place in the gourd and then hung to the horn of the saddle which exactly balanced it as the loop could not slip where it was fastened around the small place in the gourd. After the two Mexicans passed on, Wallace remarked to someone who was with him that "those fellows must have come from a dry country if God made such gourds as that for people to carry water in." These gourds were in demand by travelers and years after this, while Wallace was living in the west, he planted one of these gourd seeds in a rich place and sold twenty dollars and fifty cents worth of them from one vine. They were, however, hard to clean on account of the peculiar shape of the gourd, as it would not do to break them. All the bitter stuff and seed had to come out at the small mouth. Wallace however devised a plan to clean them without much trouble. He noticed that a great many large red ants were around his place, and that they were very fond of sweet things and would work very diligently carrying such things, so he concluded that he would make them clean his gourds. When the gourds were thoroughly dry until the seed would rattle in them, he poured a quantity of molasses or wet sugar into each and then awaited results. The ants soon discovered the sweet deposit and at once began to explore the gourds and bring out the seed at the mouthpiece which had been cut off to the hollow and which left an entrance the size of the mouth of an ordinary canteen. The consequence of this was that in time every gourd was cleaned, not a seed or fibre were left inside, and was ready to drink water out of.

Wallace and a party who came with him to San Antonio, found a boarding house and as his companions did not seem to want to ramble much as there was nothing to see, as they expressed it, Wallace said that he would go and look around and see what the country was like. He went up to the head of the San Antonio River and the springs at the head of San Pedro Creek and explored the irrigation ditches. When he returned to his companions, he told them that this was the finest country he ever saw, that if it did not rain they had the ditches already cut and full of water to irrigate with and that in his rounds saw plenty of deer which were snorting at him all the time.

Wallace stayed in San Antonio until 1839 and during that time took trips around and killed many deer. All he had to do, he says, to get a deer was to go out soon in the morning and kill as many as he wanted along the San Pedro Creek, west of town. All the settlements and houses were down on the river, except the old Catholic church, which was then, and still stands, about half way between the river and San Pedro Creek. He kept his boarding house well supplied with venison. The Indians were then hostile, and made many raids into town, and killed and carried off Mexican captives, which then constituted a very large majority of the inhabitants of San Antonio. On all occasions a sentinel was kept in the tower of the Catholic church to look out for Indians who could be seen coming a long distance across the then open country in daylight, and when such was the case, the man at the church rang the bell to notify the people of the danger, so they could all get indoors who were out, and those away from town and in hearing of the bell could run in. Sometimes the Indians would come in the night and remain on the outskirts until daylight, and then make a sudden onset upon those who had stepped out of their houses and kill or carry off such as they could. The Mexicans were poorly armed and could make but an indifferent fight with them. On one occasion, early in the morning, Wallace left the boarding house and went to pick dewberries over near the Alamo. His landlady was a Mexican, and he cannot now remember how to spell her name, but the house was on the river west of the Alamo. While picking the berries he heard the bell ring at the church, but not knowing its significance, paid no attention to it. A Mexican woman however saw him from a house near by and putting her head out of a window cried, "Correr, correr; Los Indios! los Indios! Not knowing what this meant, as he had as yet not learned the Spanish language, he kept on until he got all the berries he wanted. On returning, he asked the hostess what "Correr los Indios" meant, and was informed that it meant "Run! Indians!" He then learned that a raid had been made on that side of town and that two women had been captured and a boy wounded. Wallace was so near to them that he could hear the women crying that were being carried off. On another occasion he was out of town, and hearing the bell, at once made tracks back into town, but found out that this bell was for calling the people to church, so he said that when he heard the bell he could not tell whether the Indians were coming or whether they were going to have a preaching. On one occasion while Wallace was down the river hunting he saw a large snake trying to swallow a squirrel and had succeeded, all but head and forelegs. He shot the snake, who at once spewed up the squirrel, but the little animal was so stuck up with slime that he could not get away, but only crawl about. So Wallace picked it up and washing it clean in the river, carried it back to town and presented it to his landlady, who was proud to get it, and at once had a nice cage made for his reception. When Wallace left, there was a gay, frolicsome little squirrel, and no doubt lived a long and happy life; but would have been food for the big snake had it not been for the timely arrival of the great frontiersman, Big Foot Wallace, and his rifle.

CHAPTER V

GOING TO AUSTIN - THERE GETS THE NAME OF "BIG FOOT," TRAILING THE BIGFOOT INDIANS

In 1839, when Austin was selected to be the future capital of the young but fast growing Republic of Texas, and contracts let for building public houses, many flocked there, and wages were high for workmen. Wallace, hearing of these things, bid farewell for a season to San Antonio and at once set out for the new capital. There had been a small settlement here before, called Waterloo, but when it was selected for the capital, its name was changed to that of Austin, in honor of Stephen F. Austin who brought the colonies to Texas.

When Wallace arrived in Austin there were but few houses, but many tents and shanties, and Wallace says it seemed to him that the majority of the population were gamblers. He knew several of the citizens there, having become acquainted with them down the country before the town was started. These were Barton, Miller, Herrell and some others. There was a demand for men who could hew logs for the buildings that were being put up on both sides of Congress Avenue, and some were to build the president's house. Wallace was an expert with a broad-ax, having learned to use it well at his home in Virginia before immigrating to Texas. A man named Woods was a contractor to get out logs, and employed Wallace to hew, at a salary of two hundred dollars per month and board. He worked at this two months and then went to rafting logs of cedar from high up the river, where good logs could be found in the flats near the river. When the last load was being put on that Wallace carried down, he became worn and thirsty pitching logs off a bluff, and going down to a spring to get water, soon discovered there had been Indians there getting water, and also saw tracks where they had stood behind some trees and watched him pitch logs off the bluff. Going back to the raft, he informed his partner, William Leggett, of the situation and said they must load and get away from there before dark, as the Indians had found them out now and it would not be safe for two of them to remain there another night. By hard work the raft was loaded, they pushed off before night, and dropping down the river three miles, tied up under a bluff where no one could approach them, remained until morning, and then went on down to town all right. Wallace would not go back any more to bring logs, as he had enough of the business anyhow; but some Germans went up after logs and were all killed by the Indians. Shortly after this Wallace came near being killed in a well. His partner, Leggett, had let a bucket fall into Treasurer Brigham's well and had to get it out, so he got Wallace to help him. They got a tub and fastening the rope to it, Wallace told Leggett to get in the tub and he would let him down. "No," said he, "I will let you down." "But," said Wallace, "I am too heavy for you to hold, but I can let you down all right." Leggett contended that he could hold him all right, and finally Wallace got in the tub and started down. As Wallace feared, he gave out and let loose. Down went the tub at a most terrific rate to the bottom. In the descent Wallace skinned his face and hands against the sides of the well and landed in water up to his shoulders. He then discovered that there were not less than seven snakes in there, which were swimming all around him. The tub was split all to pieces, and seizing one of these fragments, Wallace beat off the snakes and killed them, and escaped being bitten. While this was going on Leggett looked in the well and sang out, "Are you killed?" Wallace said, "No, I have got life enough left to kill you when I get out of here." "What shall I do?" says Leggett. "Go", says Wallace, "and bring Asa Brigham's negro here to pull me out." This was at once done and the negro pulled him out. Wallace, looking around, said: "Where is Leggett?" "He's gone," replied the negro.

Austin was on the extreme frontier and nothing but one great wilderness beyond, in which Wallace delighted. It best suited his roving disposition and hermit-like nature. He loved the wild woods and gloried in all the primeval scenes of nature. Her lofty rock and cedar-capped mountains, deep canyons, dark brakes and forests, clear springs and swift rushing river, the deer, turkey, buffalo, wild horses and the painted savage, all had charms for him. He would take extensive rambles up the Colorado and then make wide circles back to the settlement, shooting game by the way and eating and sleeping when inclination came to do so.

In Austin at this time was a good-natured, jolly Irishman named William Fox. He and Wallace formed a partnership, and renting a house in town kept "bach" there together. They took contracts for jobs, one of which was to haul rock from the mountains to build houses and made lots of money. Also in this country at that time was a famous Indian called "Bigfoot," who gave the settlers great trouble, killing whoever he could, and stealing horses and other property. He was a wily rascal and the whites tried in vain to catch him. His tracks measured fourteen inches with his moccasins on, and he was large in proportion, being six feet and eight inches in height. He would come into

Austin at night and go from place to place. The next morning his track was plainly to be seen in the sandy soil. Many miles had Wallace trailed him, trying to come up with him and get a shot, but in vain. Wallace could pick out his track from a hundred—one way by its size and another was that the big toe in his right moccasin was always out and showed its imprint in the soil. He had been wounded in the knee once by a settler named Tom Green, which caused him to step awkward and caused this toe to wear a hole in the moccasin sooner than any other place. It is believed by some that Wallace got the name of "Big Foot" for killing this Indian. When being interviewed by the writer of this history, the question was asked if it was so, and he said, "No, Westfall killed him on the Llano. I trailed him many times and saw him three times at a distance, but never got a shot at him."

Then said I: "There is another story in circulation; that the Mexicans gave you that name while a prisoner in their hands in Mexico, after the battle of Mier, because they could not find a pair of shoes big enough for you in the City of Mexico."

"No," said he, "that is not so. There were men in the command who had larger feet than I. The Mexicans all have small feet and they could not find shoes large enough for any of us. My feet are not large in proportion to my body. See?" and he held them out for my inspection, and it was even so. "No. 9-1/2 or 10's", he said, "fit easy." If his feet had been smaller they would have been out of proportion to his massive frame. "But," the old man continued, "I did get my name from the Bigfoot Indian—but not because I killed him."

The story is this: One night in 1839, the Bigfoot Indian came into the town of Austin, and in prowling around, went into the kitchen of man named Gravis, and then went on up to the house where Wallace and Fox lived. Next morning Gravis trailed the Indian to their door and without trying to trace it any further, roused up Wallace and said it was him who had been in his kitchen. Wallace also wore moccasins and made a large track, but he was so incensed at Gravis, that he was about to whip him on the spot, but the latter got out of the way and told Wallace to prove himself clear and there would be no need to fight. Wallace said he could do that and at once went and placed his foot, with the moccasin on, in the Indian's track, and made Gravis come up close enough to look at it, and showed him how much longer the Indian's track was than his. This was convincing to Gravis and he apologized to Wallace and went off. During this episode, however, Fox had come to the door and was listening to all that was being said. While Wallace was standing in the big track and calling Gravis up to look at it, the Irishman laughed and said, "Now, Wallace, when the Bigfoot Indian is not around, I will call you Bigfoot." Others took up the name and sometimes when a man would say "Bigfoot," meaning likely the Indian, another would ask which one was meant, the Indian or Bigfoot Wallace. So the name has stuck to him since and has been famous along the border for half a century. After the controversy with Gravis was settled, Wallace got his gun and took up the trail of Bigfoot and followed it far into the mountains, but could not come upon him. He had to return, like many times before, empty-handed.

CHAPTER VI

HUNTING IN THE MOUNTAINS
KILLING AN INDIAN AT MT. BONNELL

Eleven miles above Austin, on the Colorado, there is a noted place called Mt. Bonnell. The name was derived from the publisher of a paper in Austin, who, with his friends, occasionally went up there for the purpose of hunting and recreation. The paper was called the "Intelligencer," and was owned and edited by William Bonnell. He lost his life in the famous Mier Expedition. In the fall of 1839 Wallace was alone on one of his long rambles and came to the base of the famous mountain where he met with one of his many exciting adventures. This mountain comes in between Cypress Creek on the east and the Colorado River on the west, ending abruptly against the river on one side and Cypress on the other. The rock walls tower high on both sides and is one of the grandest and most romantic places in all the country. On the side next to the river there is a narrow passway which curves around with the river, and which a man can safely pass by being careful and hugging close to the cliff. A mis-step, or slip, would carry him into the river, fifty feet or more below, and there is no chance for two persons coming in opposite directions to pass each other. From time immemorial, almost, this had been a great rendezvous for Indians. They had passed around this cliff in single file so often that a smooth pathway had been worn. When Wallace in his rambles came to this path, he at once began to follow it in order to save a long, tedious trip around the mountain the other way. Being by this time a cautious frontiersman, he kept his rifle ready in his right hand, and moved slowly and carefully around. Upon arriving at a point where the trail made a curve around the face of the cliff, and when he could see a few feet ahead, he was greatly surprised, and somewhat alarmed for a moment, by coming face to face with an Indian, and only a few feet apart. The Indian was also greatly surprised, and for a few seconds each gazed at the other without uttering a word. In all emergencies Wallace thought and acted quickly. If the Indian had sprung at him before he could have brought his rifle up, both would certainly have fallen over the cliff together; but he took in the situation at a glance, and punching out his rifle without taking aim, fired. The Indian had slightly turned, as if about to make an attempt to escape, when the loud report of the big rifle echoed among the cliffs and reverberated through the deep gorges and dark canyons for miles around. The daring hunter at once turned and as hastily as possible began to retrace his steps. The unfortunate savage, who had received a death shot, plunged headlong from the path, and before the sound of the gun had ceased to echo, his body was heard to strike the water below. Not knowing how many Indians might be following the one he shot, Wallace continued his flight away from the spot even when he was clear of the dangerous trail. He ran against a grapevine, which caught him under the chin and almost cut his throat and broke his neck, on account of the weight of his body and the velocity with which he was carrying it. Disengaging himself, however, from the treacherous vine, he continued his flight, and making a wide circle around the mountain, got back to Austin without further incident. It was a fortunate thing for him that he did get back, for Bigfoot was in that vicinity, and it was one of Bigfoot's warriors that Wallace had killed. These Indians belonged to the Wacoes. Wallace raised a party of seven men at Austin and next day went back to the scene of his adventure. There they discovered the trail of Bigfoot and his band, and found where they had pulled the dead Indian out of the water and carried him off, but their trail was lost among the rocks to the north of Mt. Bonnell.

When Austin was first settled, water was scarce in town until wells could be dug to supply it. Wallace dug the first well that was dug in the new capital. A saloon keeper named H. L. Savory had to pay high for water, and said he would pay $12 per foot, sand or rock, to anyone who could get him plenty. Wallace took the job, and at once went to work. He struck water at a depth of 19 feet, and so strong was the vein when he dug into it, that the water flew up in his face and he cried out: "Draw me up quick, before I drown in here." Nearly everybody in town came to look at the water and brought their buckets to get some of it. The well was on Congress Avenue, on the corner of Pine Street. It is still in existence, the best well in the city, and goes by the name of "Wallace Well."

There were many buffalo in the vicinity of Austin in those days, especially north of town, where there were no roads or little traveling except by hunters and Indians. One day Wallace was out in that direction, and seeing a herd of eleven buffalo, tried to get a shot at them. But they, keen-scented animals that they are, got wind of him and ran in the direction of town, and he followed them in a lively chase. At this time the city of Austin was being laid off, and stakes had been driven along both sides of Congress Avenue, designating streets, sidewalks, etc., commencing from capital hill. The stakes had little red flags tied to them, and when the buffalo came over the hill, they took down towards the river between these stakes, turning their shaggy heads and eyeing the red flags suspiciously as they passed. Wallace and his buffalo created such a noise and dust as they entered town, that all the people ran out to see what was the matter, and some of the men tried to head them off, but the big game would not turn, and they had to give way to them and let them pass. The bluff on the river south of town was very high and steep, and the water deep below. When the buffalo arrived here they made no halt, but at once leaped off, and the splashing they made when they hit the water was heard by the people in town. The buffalo were not hurt, and swam straight across the river, their black heads up and looking like huge sea monsters. In this manner the last buffalo that made a track in Austin were run through there by "Bigfoot" Wallace.

Wallace made a great amount of money selling meat in town to those who did not hunt, or were too busy or afraid to leave town. One load of turkeys and bear that he brought in once sold for $70. Another man named Reinhart, and his partner Ladd, also hunted and would go out with a wagon and yoke of oxen to bring in their game. Wallace told them that some day the Indians would get them, but they still plied their trade, as they were making money. One time, however, the Indians came, but they saw them in time to leave their wagon and run. Reinhart got away tolerably easy, but Ladd's boots were too big for him and he could not run good. They crowded him close until they ran him out of his boots and then they fell behind. When his heavy boots came off, he said he felt so light he could almost fly; and getting into a drift near the river, hid, and they could not find him. The Indians went back to the wagon, and killing both of the oxen, scalped them, taking off the hide from the forehead. They had a dog with them, but he got lost in the chase. Wallace and several others went back to the wagon when they heard the news and found the dog in the wagon and a gang of buzzards around the dead oxen. Ladd was with the crowd and the dog was greatly delighted to see him. A man named Rogers was with Reinhart and Ladd when the Indians chased them, but he, being horseback, had left the wagon just before the chase and gone off in quest of game. Not coming in, it was feared the Indians had killed him, which afterwards proved to be true. The party searched for him and it was the evening of the second day before the body was found in a ravine not more than half a mile from the wagon. The searchers were attracted to the spot by buzzards. By this time such a stench was coming from the body that most of the men recoiled and the horses tried to run away from the spot. At first no one seemed inclined to bury the unfortunate man. Finally Wallace said there was no use talking, he had to be buried, and if no one would help, he would do it alone. Dismounting, he tied his horse, pulled his heavy bowie knife and commenced digging by the side of the body. One man named Jack Angel came to his assistance and they soon covered him up. They now went on the trail of Ladd's flight and found his boots. All this occurred about twenty miles from Austin, out towards the San Gabriel.

Wallace says that during his stay around Austin, more than forty people were killed by Indians, and he helped bury twenty-two of them. Most of these killings were by Bigfoot and his gang. There were but eight of them. Of these Wallace killed one, Tom Malone another and Tom Green wounded Bigfoot himself in the knee. Then they left that country and were next heard of in the southwest in the Frio and Nueces country.

On one occasion the saloon keeper, Savory, had some flour on hand and employed Wallace one night to watch it, for fear someone would steal it. Wallace went to sleep and sure enough, when he awoke about daylight, one barrel was gone. He determined to find the thief and flour if there was any chance, and set out on the trail. Fortune favored him in this for the barrel had a hole in it and the flour sifted out as he moved along, leaving a thin, white trail on the ground. Finally, however, he came to where the flour had been put into two sacks, evidently the thief having met a partner here. Still luck was on the side of the trailer, for both sacks had holes in them and left plenty sign. This trail led to where an immigrant had stopped a few days before and who had some negroes. Wallace asked the man if he had any flour to sell. He said no, that he had just bought some himself from a man who had some to sell, and who was there before it was good light. On the question being asked if he would know the man again if he could see him, he said yes. The trail of the other sack was now taken, and it led to a saw pit in the edge of town, where two men were found asleep. One of them was awakened and was asked who brought the flour there. He pointed to the other man, whose name was Snelling, and said that he was the man. This fellow had his head covered up. Wallace pulled the quilt off, and taking him by the collar marched him off to the office of the Justice of the Peace. This official was very ignorant and uneducated. He had been a log rafter, and the gamblers, who ruled the town, had elected him for sport. The case, however, was tried before him, and after patiently listening to all the evidence, bound Snelling over to keep the peace. Court broke up in an uproar of mirth, and Savory would not have any of his flour back. Wallace says that beat any decision in a court of justice that he ever heard of, binding a man over to keep the peace for stealing a barrel of flour.

CHAPTER VII

SEVERE SICKNESS OF WALLACE - LIVING IN A CAVE - WILLIAM FOX KILLED BY THE BIGFOOT INDIANS.

About the latter part of 1839 a flux broke out among the people of Austin and a great many of them died. Wallace says this was caused by a lot of soldiers being sent there, for it first appeared among them and then spread everywhere. He was afflicted also and came near dying, but an old French lady named Tetar saved him. She parched flour until it was brown and then boiled milk. Mixing the two into a thin mush, she gave him a teaspoonful at a time until the malady was stopped. Captain Wallace said that the time he was taken sick he was engaged to be married, but when he began to recover from his sickness, the hair on his head all came out, and, as he says, "was a nice looking chap to get married," so he determined that when he got able, to take to the mountains and stay there until his hair grew out again. He was also tired, he says, of lying on the porch where he lived and seeing dead people carried by; and hearing the dead march played, and hearing it remarked about him that "that fellow toughs it out well; they haven't carried him to the bone yard yet!" People scattered from town in all directions and General Houston had the soldiers sent away. Then the disease began to abate and soon died out.

As soon as "Bigfoot" Wallace was able to travel, he told Fox, his partner, to get things ready — horses, guns, blankets, provisions, ammunition, etc.

—and they would be off. This was soon done and they wended their way up the Colorado, and made a camp near the mouth of a cave at the foot of Mount Bonnell. Here Wallace said he would stay and hunt while Fox took the horses back to town, but for he (Fox) to come back every Saturday after the meat and see how he was getting along. He soon began to gain strength and killed three bears before the week was out, besides other game. It was the best place for game, he says, that he ever saw. It was the great crossing and watering place for all kinds of game, from one side of the river to the other. He moved his bedding and other things inside the cave and slept there, as it was a good place to stand off a bunch of Indians. The cave was cool and also a capital place to save meat. The bear which he had killed were very fat, and having plenty of bear grease, greased his bald head every day, after which he would wash it all off with soap, in the river. In a short time he said his head was covered with a fine soft down that looked like a young buzzard, and would often wonder, as he gazed into the looking glass, if he would ever have any hair again. He kept up his greasing, however, and in a short time the "fuzz" all came off, and then, sure enough, hair began to come. His strength was returning and he felt that soon "Richard would be himself again." The Irishman came regularly every Saturday night and brought such things as he was in need of — newspapers, etc. Fox always arrived in the night when Wallace was in his cave, and his first greeting would be, "Hello! Bigfoot, are you dead?" The next day he would pack his horses with meat and wend his way back, never carrying any gun or pistol. Wallace often told him that he would meet his death some day at the hands of the Indians.

One night upon Fox's arrival, after asking Wallace if he was dead, and being answered in the negative, he says: "Well, then, be Jasus, Captain, I have got bad news for you. What do you think? Your sweetheart has gone and married another man."

"I am glad she's gone," says Wallace. "A woman that can't wait until a man's hair grows out I don't want."

The writer asked the old Captain if he ever married. "No," he replied, contemptuously, "I never had time."

As near as he ever came to kissing a woman, he says, was while he was prisoner in Mexico, with his hands tied behind him. He bit an old Mexican woman on the back of the neck for making faces at him.

Captain Wallace says although he has been a powerful man physically, there were three things he could never do, namely: whistle, sing or dance. These accomplishments were beyond his reach.

After "Bigfoot" had recovered his health and his black, curly hair had come out profusely again, he returned to town and he and Fox again took up their abode as of yore.

Not long after this, Fox hired to Asa Brigham to help his negro break up a garden down near Shoal Creek in the suburbs of town. The negro held the plow while Fox drove the oxen. The trail of the Bigfoot Indian had not been seen around Austin for a long time and it was surmised by some that he had been killed somewhere, but this was not so. He was even now secreted behind the brush fence which enclosed the garden, gun in hand, waiting a chance to shoot at Fox and the negro. Finally the Irishman stopped the team to take a chew of tobacco, and as the plug was between his teeth, a gun was fired from the fence and he fell dead in his tracks, shot through the head. The negro took one look in the direction from whence came the shot, saw the smoke floating above the brush, saw a tall form of an Indian standing behind it, and then leaped the fence and fled.

When the news was carried to town, Wallace at once got his gun and a few followers and hurriedly went down where Fox lay, took one look at his dead friend who lay with the tobacco still between his teeth, and then took the trail of the big Indian. Long and diligently he followed him this time, but of no avail. He once more made his escape. Fox was shot in the temple and the ball came out on the other side. He was also scalped, all being taken close behind the ears. No doubt the Indian dressed this scalp and prized it highly, for it was beautiful —thick, long, coal black and curly. It is a little strange that William Fox, the man who gave to Wallace the name of "Bigfoot," was afterwards killed and scalped by the Bigfoot Indian.

In 1840, Col. John H. Moore organized an expedition against the Indians and had a severe battle with them on the San Saba River, in which they were defeated; many being killed and drowned together in attempting to cross the river. Two Indian boys were captured and brought to Austin and one of them was taken by the French minister and kept for a servant. The Frenchman had so much confidence in this young savage that he would let him go alone and ride one of his fine matched carriage horses (beautiful greys) and lead the other to water at the river. Wallace told him that some day the young Comanche would go back to the west and take the horses with him. No, the Frenchman did not believe this, but said that when he went back to France he would carry the Indian with him and educate him. Not long after this, the Indian took the horses and left. The minister fumed and sputtered around at a great rate. Wallace told him not to take on, as the young Indian had concluded to finish his education on the plains instead of Paris,

and, no doubt, would be promoted as soon as he got back to his tribe with the fine horses.

CHAPTER VIII

INDIAN RAID AND BATTLE OF BRUSHY CREEK - A BRAVE BOY.

During the sojourn of Captain Wallace in Austin, he took a trip back to LaGrange, and while there heard of the Indian raid near Austin in which Mrs. Coleman and one of her sons were killed, and the house of Dr. Robinson plundered, and some of his negroes carried off. The doctor and family was absent at the time and therefore escaped. As soon as the news came to the settlement at LaGrange of the raid, Wallace and about twenty others at once started for Austin to assist in routing the hostiles, who were Comanches and in large force. When they arrived at Mrs. Coleman's place, they saw her dead body and that of her son. The brave boy had killed one Indian in his gallant defense of his mother and his younger brothers and sisters. They were forted up in their log cabin and he and his mother were firing on the Indians through the cracks between the logs. The Indians also shot their arrows through these cracks. The mother fell first, pierced with an arrow, and died at once. The boy continued the defense until he fell mortally wounded. When dying, he told his sister that he would not groan, as the Indians would then not know he was hurt. The savages left without entering the house and the balance of the family were saved.

Wallace and his party learned here that the Indians had turned north and gone in the direction of Brushy Creek and that a force under Gen. Edward Burleson had started in pursuit of them. Being anxious to participate in the battle, if any should come off, they set out on the trail, but were too late. Burleson and his men had engaged the Indians on Brushy Creek, twenty miles away, and were returning. The two parties met at Wilbarger's house, where quite a number of settlers had fortified themselves. Although the Indians had been defeated in the battle, the settlers did not return unscathed — four of their party having been killed, besides others wounded. The dead were: Jacob Burleson, brother of the General; James Gilleland, a Methodist preacher; Lemuel Blakey and ___ Walters. When the men slowly arrived bearing their gallant dead, Captain Wallace says such a wail went up from the women assembled that he could not stand it and left the house. Shortly after, he and his party went on to the battleground to see what discoveries they could make. Many signs of the battle were there in the ravine where the Indians fought. While searching around, Wallace heard someone groaning in a ravine near by. On investigating, he found one of Dr. Robinson's negroes who had been wounded in the forehead by an arrow and the spike still remained fast in the skull. He had been left there when the Indians retreated. He complained very much and said he thought the wound would kill him. Wallace pulled the arrow out of his head and told him to hush, saying: "Whoever heard of a negro being killed, shot in the head?" The negro could not tell much about the fight as he was shot at the commencement of the action, as prisoners generally are by Indians. He had then laid close in the ravine and kept quiet during the time and until they left. He was carried back home and recovered.

Captain Wallace says that shortly after coming to Texas, he was stopping one night with a man named Woods, who lived twelve miles above La-Grange. Before bedtime, another man came and before taking his seat at the fire, pulled off the cap which he wore. Wallace noticed that his head was bald and sore, and remarked: "My friend, excuse me, but what is the matter with your head?" "I have been scalped by Indians," he replied. This man was Josiah Wilbarger, and his experience would make a thrilling chapter in Texas history. The circumstance, as near as could be learned, was this: Wilbarger and Joe Hornsby, and a few others, were out one day and came in contact with a band of Indians. Not being strong enough to make a good fight, they began to retreat. Wilbarger was soon wounded and unhorsed, and made a stand beside a tree to fight. Hornsby pulled up his horse and made a halt beside him, firing on the Indians as they came around, but his companion received another wound and fell. Hornsby, one of the bravest of the brave, saw there was no chance to save him, and putting spurs to his horse, saved himself. When he arrived at home, the news was soon spread and a crowd of men collected at Hornsby's that night for the purpose of fighting the Indians and bringing in the body of Wilbarger in the morning. Joe Hornsby was a young man without family and lived with his widowed mother. During the night a strange thing happened. Mrs. Hornsby dreamed that Wilbarger was not dead but was in great distress, and insisted on Joe getting up and at once repairing to the spot to assist him. He, however, insisted that it was impossible for Josiah to have survived and suggested that they wait until the morning. This dream was repeated twice more during the night and each time the anxious and good woman aroused her son and begged him to go to the wounded man. Joe said: "Mother, it is your excited and overstrained imagination that causes you to dream these things. Wilbarger is dead. The last I saw of him he was down on his back, and the Indians were running their lances through him. They never quit a man as long as there is any life in him." His mother, however, was not convinced, and said that she could see the tree and described all the surroundings. He was not there, but had gone to a water hole. By daylight next morning, the men were in the saddle and ready to start, but Hornsby's mother insisted on Joe taking a blanket with which to make a stretcher to convey Wilbarger on, "for," says she, "he is not dead." When the party arrived at the spot, guided by Hornsby, who was the last man to see him and who knew where to search, they were surprised to discover that the body was not there. There was plenty of blood and a trail led away from the tree, which on being followed, soon led to a pool of water in which the wounded man was found. He was not dead, but horribly wounded and scalped. No time was lost in getting him out and conveying him on the blanket stretched between two horses, to Mrs. Hornsby's, who, when they arrived, was not at all surprised, but had everything prepared for his reception. Wilbarger says that soon after Hornsby left him, he felt the lances of the Indians thrust in him, but was so weak from loss of blood from the other wounds that he had received, that he was almost unconscious, and was entirely unable to make any resistance, and lay still. After this he felt a knife working around over his head and knew that an Indian was scalping him. When the skin was cut loose all around the top of his head to the bone, the Indian twisted the hair in his fingers and with one strong jerk brought the scalp off. He said when this was done it sounded like a gun had been fired in his ear and he soon became unconscious. How long this lasted he could not tell, but when consciousness returned again, it was like waking up from a sleep. He opened his eyes and looked around but at first could hardly realize the situation. The moon was shining, and he rested his eyes on a figure, as he thought, sitting beside the tree looking at him. What made him feel stranger still was the fact that the figure was that of his sister who had been dead many years and had never been to Texas. This vision vanished soon and he began to realize all that had happened to him, by his head burning like fire, where his scalp had been taken off. He thought of the waterhole near by, and felt that if he could get to it and dip his head under, it would relieve and cool it. When he made the attempt to get there, however, he was so badly wounded that he was unable to rise and could but barely crawl along, and then only with great pain. He succeeded, however, in getting there. Crawling into the pond, he dipped his head under which greatly relieved him. He repeated this whenever his head began to burn, until the arrival of the rescuers. He recovered and lived many years. This statement was vouched for by all who were concerned and present on that occasion, as long as any of the participants lived.

CHAPTER IX

CAPTURE OF SAN ANTONIO BY THE MEXICANS.

We come now to the period in the life of "Bigfoot" Wallace when he began to serve the young Republic in the capacity of a Texas Ranger under the famous Jack Hays who stands preeminently at the head of that long list of ranger captains.

In 1840 the situation around San Antonio, which was then on the extreme frontier, was anything but encouraging to those who wished to settle in the country and lead quiet lives and make good citizens. Besides the constant raids of the numerous bands of Indians who roamed at will from the line of New Mexico to the coast region of Texas, horse thieves, desperadoes, gamblers and fugitives from justice, who had fled from other states, swarmed around all the border towns, and more especially San Antonio. No one was safe who was in opposition to this element, and to keep horses was impossible. They would dig through adobe houses to get to them. No place was safe from their encroachments.

A strong hand was needed here to awe this class and hold them in subjection. There was one man in West Texas at this time who was equal to the emergency. That was Jack Hays, a young surveyor who had already begun to make himself known and felt, especially at the battle of Plum Creek, where 500 Comanche warriors had been defeated after they had made a raid through Texas and burned and plundered the town of Linnville on the coast.

Gen. Houston recognized the ability of Hays, and seeing the necessity of an armed, active force at San Antonio, to hold both Indians and lawless characters in check, commissioned Jack Hays to raise a company to be stationed at San Antonio as headquarters. Hays was to follow horse thieves or Indians anywhere he wished and to shoot horse thieves on the spot, if necessary, when overtaken.

In 1840 "Bigfoot" Wallace left Austin and went back to San Antonio and joined the company of Hays when it was organized. Captain Hays was very particular what kind of men he enlisted and that is one reason why he had the best set of Indian fighters on the frontier. He was never defeated by the Indians. A man had to have courage, good character, be a good rider, good shot, and have a horse worth $100. Among the first company were Wallace, Woolfork, Joe Tivey, Mark Rapier, Kit Ackland, Jim Galbreth, Tom Buchanan, Coho Jones, Peter Poe, Mike Chevalier, Ad Gillespie and others not now remembered. Among those who came later, and followed the fortunes of Hays, and helped to fight his battles and gain a reputation for him as an Indian fighter, which is almost worldwide, were Sam Walker, Sam Luckey, George Neill, James Dunn, Ben McCulloch, Henry McCulloch, Ben Highsmith, Tom Galbreth, Andrew Sowell, John Sowell, P.H. Bell, Creed Taylor, Sam Cherry, Noah Cherry, John Carlin, Rufus Perry, Joe Davis, Pipkin Taylor, Josiah Taylor, Rufus Taylor, James Nichols, Calvin Turner, Lee Jackson, and many other gallant men whose names cannot now be obtained. Captain Wallace says that the Woolfork mentioned in the first list of rangers was a brother-in-law of Governor L. S. Ross's father, and that Joe Tivey was afterwards mayor of Kerrville, and was one of the best men he ever saw.

Not long after Wallace joined the rangers, one morning he went into a Mexican restaurant and called for breakfast. A woman soon brought him coffee, bread, etc., and a small animal broiled whole on the coals, which look fat and tempting, and said: "Cara cerreo, senior?" Wallace did not know very much of the Spanish language at that time and nodded assent, thinking likely the little animal was a squirrel or rabbit. He soon found it was neither, but being palatable, made a hearty meal, eating all but the head. As he was stepping out of the eating house, he met Jim Dunn, another ranger, who understood the Spanish and asked him what "Cerreo" meant. Dunn said, "That means a polecat." "What!" said Wallace. "Did that damned woman give me a polecat to eat?" Dunn then stepped in and asked if she had given this man a polecat for breakfast. "Oh, yes," she said, in Spanish, "he is very fond of them, and ate a whole one, all but the head." This settled it with "Bigfoot," he had nothing more to say and stepped out.

During the years 1840-41, Hays and his men captured many horse thieves in and around San Antonio and shot several of them. On one occasion they captured a notorious one named Antonio Corao. Four of the company were detailed to shoot him, namely: "Bigfoot" Wallace, Chapman Woolfork, Sam Walker and William Powell. The execution took place at the head of the San Antonio River, above town. Many years after this Wallace was in San Antonio sitting with a crowd of men at the Southern Hotel, when a Mexican, apparently very drunk, came up and said to "Bigfoot," "Are you "Bigfoot" Wallace?" "Yes," was the reply, "what do you want?" The Mexican then came up close, looked Wallace in the face and said, "You helped to kill Antonio Corao and he was a friend of mine." "He was?" exclaimed Wallace, as he sprang to his feet and pulled his knife, "I want to kill all his friends, too!" By this time the Mexican was making tracks and "Bigfoot" after him. The Mexican was not as drunk as he seemed and outran Wallace and made his escape. He barely missed getting a slash from the long-bladed knife, and likely would have gotten it if some friends had not caught Wallace by the arm and impeded his progress.

The rangers under Hays, while stationed in San Antonio and vicinity, were very active scouting far and near and fighting several battles with the Indians. Things went on in this way until the fall of 1842 when the Mexicans under General Adrian Woll made a sudden descent upon San Antonio and captured the place. Prior to this event, however, there was a suspicion that something was wrong, from the fact that all at once no ammunition could be bought in San Antonio by the Americans, it having all been bought up at various times by the Mexicans. Wallace told Captain Hays that he saw at least a dozen strange Mexicans in town that he had never seen before who did not live there. The nearest place where ammunition could be obtained was Austin, and thither Hays sent Wallace and another ranger named Nathaniel Mallon to get a supply. Mallon was afterwards sheriff of Bexar county and the first one, Captain Wallace says.

When they arrived at Austin there was considerable excitement there on account of an Indian raid in which Captain William Pyron and another man named Donovan were killed. The bodies had not been brought in and some were afraid to venture out of town to get them. Wallace and his companion said they would go and soon others volunteered and a hack load started out. Donovan was with a man named Herrill out after hay when the Indians made the attack upon them. Herrill was armed and kept the Indians at bay while his team ran into town with him sitting on the load. Donovan had a cart and was killed. Captain Pyron was interested in the hay and had gone there on horseback. The Indians overtook him and one of them

ran a lance in him, but the Captain caught it and wrenched it out of the Indian's hand. Pulling it out of his own body, it seems that he fought the Indian with it, for here the Indian turned back, but Pyron had received a mortal wound and falling from his horse, died. The lance, with the blade bent, was lying by his side when Wallace and his party came with the hack to take him up. The Irishman, Donovan, had made a fight and emptied his gun. He was both shot and lanced. The bodies lay north of town from one and one-half to two miles distant. Pyron was on his race mare and could have made his escape, but remained with the others until it was too late. The Indians got his fine nag and saddle.

The two rangers, after helping to bury the dead men, obtained their ammunition and started back to San Antonio. Wallace had a full keg of powder rolled up in a blanket and fastened to the pommel of his saddle, and Mallon had a supply of caps and lead. As there was no settlement between Austin and San Antonio, they went back by way of Seguin to get corn for their horses as they had rode hard and the grass was coarse and dry. In the meantime the Mexicans had captured San Antonio. It was a fine thing for them that they went by Seguin, for otherwise they would have rode into San Antonio and been captured and their ammunition taken. The first ranch on the Austin road in the vicinity of Seguin was that of Antonio Navarro, on the San Geronimo Creek, about six miles distant from town. What was their surprise on coming to this place to find two of Hays' men, (Rice and Johnson) there, and the Mexican woman picking prickly pear thorns out of them. As soon as Wallace saw them he said, "Hello, boys, what are you doing here?" They now gave an account of the capture of San Antonio and of the narrow escape of the rangers who were badly scattered. These two had been run closely through the pears and thorny brush by the Mexican cavalry, but had made their escape to the Guadalupe River and crossed. Captain Hays and some of the men were on a scout when the Mexican army came into town. They could not enter again and came on east of the Salado, went into camp and sent runners to notify the settlers at Seguin and Gonzales. Some of the rangers who were in their quarters in town were captured, and all of the camp equipage that belonged to the company. When the attack was made they had a fight, and could not do much, but killed General Woll's horse and the band master in the skirmish. One ranger named William Mason ran out and made his escape by running through a squad of cavalry who gave way to him as he came flourishing a pistol. As soon as Wallace and his companion could get something to eat for themselves and feed for their horses, they went on to Seguin. When they arrived there the town was full of men from Gonzales and other places on their way to fight the Mexicans. They were all short of powder and when they found out that Wallace had a keg, they wanted to take it, but he told them that no one got that powder except Jack Hays, or by his order, and he would shoot the first man that laid hands on it. In a short time, however, Hays and his lieutenant, Henry McCulloch, arrived in town and taking charge of the ammunition, divided it out. Wallace said to the men, "You are a fine lot of frontiersmen; got a rifle and nothing to feed it on." This powder and lead arrived at a very opportune time, as the battle of Salado could not have been fought without it, so says Captain Wallace. An advance was now made upon San Antonio led by General Matthew Caldwell, who had arrived with the men from Gonzales. The incidents that followed and the battle of Salado will be given in the next chapter.

CHAPTER X

BATTLE OF SALADO - WALLACE FIGHTS FOR A PAIR OF PANTS - RETREAT OF THE MEXICANS - FIGHT ON THE HONDO.

The news of the invasion of Texas and the capture of San Antonio by the Mexicans spread far and near and men were arming and mounting from the outside settlements on the Guadalupe to the Colorado valley, around LaGrange and Bastrop, and up to the new capital. Men started towards San Antonio as they could prepare themselves and went in companies, squads and singly. The first large force to arrive in the vicinity of the seat of war was that from the Guadalupe valley under General Caldwell, who was called by the men, "Old Paint." He was an Indian fighter and took part in the great Indian battle of Plum Creek fought in 1840 in Caldwell county, near the spot where Lockhart now stands. The scattered rangers of Hays were all collected and went under the command of Caldwell, who went into camp with his men on Salado Creek, seven miles northeast of San Antonio. Daring scouts were sent almost to the suburbs of San Antonio to watch the Mexicans and report any move on their part to Caldwell. Many of the citizens of the town had been captured, including those in attendance on the district court which was then in session. Judge, jury, lawyers, witnesses and all were now in the hands of the invaders. Among the citizens of the town who were taken were: John Twohig, afterwards a noted banker and brother-in-law of Jack Hays, Al Shelby and Col. Thomas Johnson. The latter two were citizens of Seguin, and all four married the daughters of Major Calvert of that place. Mr. Twohig had a store in San Antonio at the time of the Woll invasion but blew it up on the approach of the Mexicans. He suffered many hardships at their hands and bore the scars on his legs made by chains while in captivity to the day of his death. The policy of General Caldwell was to draw the Mexicans out of San Antonio and induce them to assail his position, which was a strong one on the banks of Salado Creek. His force was far less than that of the Mexican invader and he knew that an assault upon the town on his part would be a useless sacrifice of men. The Texans had learned to avoid being caught like rats in a trap by the Mexicans. They remembered the Alamo and Goliad. The rangers under Hays, or part of them at least, determined to bring on the battle, and boldly advanced to within half a mile of the Alamo. They were all good horsemen and well mounted. They cut many capers in plain view of the Mexicans, yelling at them and daring them to battle. Among these were Hays, H. E. McCulloch, "Bigfoot" Wallace, Sam Walker, Ad Gillespie, Kit Ackland, Sam Luckey, George Neill, Rufus Perry, Tom Galbreth, Andrew Sowell, Creed Taylor, Pipkin Taylor, Josiah Taylor, Mike Chevalier, and others not now remembered. Finally a blast of bugles and the sudden charge of four companies of cavalry upon them caused the rangers to wheel and put back across the prairie towards Caldwell. A lively fusillade commenced and lasted all the way to the creek, the rangers firing back as they ran. On this occasion "Bigfoot" Wallace was riding a mule, and a good one, but Hays told him to turn back before the charge commenced, as he would be overtaken. Wallace said, "I can beat them from Powder House Hill to camp," but turned back here and was working in the lead during the chase. Lieutenant

McCulloch, with ten men, covered the retreat of Hays, and were fired at almost 200 times during the long run, but neither man nor horse was hit. The infantry, 1200 in number, under Woll, followed with artillery. Crossing the creek below, they marched up the east bank and formed in line of battle facing Caldwell's position, and soon a general engagement was on. The Mexicans first fired with cannon, trying to run Caldwell from his position, which was in the pecan timber near the bank of the creek, but they only yelled and watched closely the falling limbs from the trees torn off by the cannon balls. Seeing this had no effect, Woll ordered a charge on their position and they came yelling like Indians, firing their escopetas. The rifles of the Texans now began to crack and many of them turned back, but others came close; almost up to the muzzles of the guns, and things were lively for a time. When the Mexicans captured the quarters of the rangers in San Antonio they got a pair of pants belonging to Wallace. When the battle was about to commence he told some of the boys that he was going to watch his chance to kill a big Mexican so that he could get a pair of pants to fit him. During this charge, when some of them were close, a daring fellow charged Wallace and presenting his escopeta, sang out in Spanish, "Take that, you damned cow-thief," and fired. The bullet grazed the ranger's nose, making it burn like fire, but doing no other damage. Wallace fired at the same time, but the smoke from the Mexican's gun blinded him and he missed. Henry Whaling, who was near and had a loaded gun, said, "Damn such shooting as that," and aiming his rifle quick, sent a ball through the Mexican's body, who fell against a mesquite tree and soon died. He was a cavalryman but had dismounted and his spurs were so large he could not run. Wallace says he never saw such large spurs. As he lay on his back his feet were elevated several inches in the air, as the rowels, which were as long as tenpenny nails, rested on the ground. Wallace took them off after the battle and kept them a long time as a curiosity. The Mexicans were repulsed. Wallace said not as many of them were killed as might have been expected, on account of a ravine which most of the Mexicans followed, both in making the charge and retreating. General Cordova and his French interpreter were both killed just across the ravine. Cordova was stirring up the Indians in Texas to fight the white settlers, and this Frenchman was his interpreter among the Cherokees. He was defeated in a battle near Seguin in 1839 by General Ed Burleson and his rangers.

During the next charge, one of the rangers said to Wallace: "'Bigfoot', yonder is a Mexican with pants large enough for you; look after him." The Mexican in question was assisting some others to carry off the dead and wounded that had fallen in the charge. Wallace was a conspicuous figure during the fight. His dress, massive frame, and actions when he was talking about the pants, attracted the notice of General Caldwell who rode up to him and said: "What command do you hold, sir?" "None," said Wallace. "I am one of Jack Hays' rangers and want that fellow's pants yonder," at the same time pointing out his intended victim. He had reloaded his rifle after firing at one and now watched for a fair shot at the big one. When it was offered, he downed him in his tracks. The Mexicans left him, as well as several others, and Wallace secured the pants which he said was of splendid material and a good fit. He wore them to Mexico in the Mier Expedition the following year.

Wallace said that after the battle, some of the men, while looking at the dead Mexicans, discovered that nearly all of them carried money of small denominations in their ears; sometimes as much as 25 or 30 cents in dimes and 5-cent pieces. The Mexican whom he killed and got the pants from had $2.75 twisted up in his sash. Wallace said when he found it: "Look here boys, how much I found in the sash; that fellow must have been a banker." The Mexicans were defeated in the battle and withdrew with loss; but how great could not be ascertained. Wallace says there were about twenty-two left in the flats in view. Of the Texans, Jett was killed and Creed Taylor, Calvin Turner and William Simms were wounded. Wallace was hit with four spent balls—three in the legs and one on the knuckle of the right hand—but only made bruises. The Mexicans did a great deal of firing at long range, and when they were close, overshot. In this battle Woll had about 1500 men, cavalry and infantry, while Caldwell's men has been variously estimated by those who were in the fight. Wallace says there were 196 white men and one negro named Tom, who had formerly belonged to General Sam Houston, but had been given his freedom. Tom wounded himself during the fight by the accidental discharge of his gun, badly tearing his hand. The writer once asked General H. E. McCulloch how many men were in the battle and he said 201. Wallace said two Mexicans deserted the Texans just before the fight. Just at the winding up of the battle, a desperate and sad tragedy occurred a short distance east of the battleground. A company of men, 52 in number, from Fayette county, and commanded by Captain Nicholas Dawson, were surrounded on the prairie by the Mexican army who had just been defeated by Caldwell, and nearly all killed, including their commander. They fought well, but had no chance. A few were taken and carried to Mexico. The Mexicans then returned to San Antonio, followed by some of the rangers to watch their movements.

Here are a few of the names of the Texans who fought at Salado: Matthew Caldwell, commander; Jack Hays, captain; Ewen Cameron, captain; H. E. McCulloch, lieutenant; Jesse Billingsley, captain; Milford Day, Creed Taylor, Solomon Brill, Ezekiel Smith, French Smith, Clay Davis, John Henry Brown, William King, John King, Henry King, James Nichols, John Nichols, Tom Galbreth, Ben Highsmith, Wilson Randle, Andrew Sowell, Calvin Turner, William Turner, Hardin Turner, Kit Ackland, "Bigfoot" Wallace, Mike Chevalier, Arch Gibson, James Clark, Miles Dikes, Henry Whaling, Rufus Perry, Sam Luckey, George Neill, Rufus Taylor, Josiah Taylor, Sam Walker, Ad Gillespie, Green McCoy, Robert Hall. There were many other gallant men in this fight, but their names cannot now be recalled.

In a few days the Mexicans began their retreat back to Mexico, carrying their prisoners with them. The Texans had been reinforced by men from the Colorado and other places, led by Colonels Burleson and Mayfield, until nearly 500 men followed the enemy from San Antonio. The rangers hung close on their rear and came into collision with them on the Hondo. Captain Hays proposed to charge the rear of the Mexicans with his rangers and capture their cannon, which had been posted on the near approach of the Texans, if the balance of the men would support the charge. This was understood and the onset made. Well did the rangers carry out their part of the program. They charged to the muzzles of the pieces and shot the gunners down around them, but the support failed to come and they had to retreat back to the main body. In this short, desperate dash, Lee Herrill's horse was killed by a grape shot and himself wounded in the foot. Arch Gibson had his cheek bone shot off and Sam Luckey was shot through with a ball and fell from his horse. This latter incident, however, took place

just before the charge was made, the shot being fired by a rifleman in ambush. "Bigfoot" Wallace was riding his mule in the charge, and when the cannon was reached was unable to control him and he dashed almost into a line of infantry which had been formed to support the battery. Wallace tried hard to pull up, but the mule kept on braying at every jump, with the balls whistling by, until one burnt the end of his nose. Then he wheeled quick and went back the other way. "Bigfoot" laid low on his neck to avoid the shots and fired back as he went. It seems the failure on the part of the other men to support the rangers was caused by a dispute as to who would lead. Wallace places the blame on Colonel Mayfield, and others on Caldwell. The writer heard General Henry E. McCulloch say that it was a disgrace to Texas history and as little as could be said about it, the better for all concerned.

The writer has visited the place where this halt of the Mexican army was made and can trace the route and locate the ground where the charge was made; not so much by signs still visible, but from the old settlers who live there, some of whom went there three years after the fight, when the cart tracks were still to be seen, and where the banks had been dug down, brush cut, etc. It was in fact a plain beaten out road and remained so for years. There were 1200 or more Mexican troops besides mules, horses and carts. There were both infantry and cavalry. The route of their retreat was about three miles north of the present settlements of Quihi and New Fountain and on nearly a west course from San Antonio, crossing the Medina above where Castroville is now. The fight took place between the Verde and Hondo, on the east side of the latter, and distant about forty miles from San Antonio. The pursuit ended here and the Texans scattered back to their several homes.

CHAPTER XI

THE SOMERVELL EXPEDITION.

"Bigfoot" Wallace remained in the service of the rangers with Hays until the famous Mier Expedition of 1843. After the invasion of Texas by General Woll, the people were greatly excited and an invasion of Mexico was freely talked of. The Indians were also committing depredations within two miles of the state capital and there was a general restless feeling all along the border. The Texans were still chafing on account of the bold invasion of the Mexicans, and although they had defeated them on the Salado, they were not satisfied with themselves for letting them escape so easily at the Hondo. Men were continually coming in from the east and concentrating west of San Antonio. On the 13th of October 1842, General Alexander Somervell received a special order from the state government to select some point in the west, there assemble the volunteers and drill them. The place selected was on the Medina River, where the forces were drilled and organized. "Bigfoot" Wallace was with these men under his old captain Jack Hays, who had joined the expedition with his rangers. On the 18th of November, General Somervell left his camp and marched with 750 men toward the Rio Grande. The command arrived at Laredo, on the Texas side of the river, on the 8th day of December. About 100 Mexicans who occupied the town crossed the river into Mexico on the approach of the Texans. The command now marched three miles down the stream and encamped. On the next day a portion of the men returned and plundered the town of

Laredo. This was against orders and some say the goods were collected and returned to the owners by Somervell.

At this time there was a great deal of dissatisfaction in camp and the commander gave permission to all those who wished to do so, to return to their homes. About 200 returned under the command of Colonel J. L. Bennett. The remainder of the command moved down and camped opposite the town of Guerrero on the 14th.

In the next two days the Texans crossed the river and advanced towards the town, camped near by, and virtually had possession of the place; but Captain Wallace says that he was the only man that entered, and that was by accident, or necessity. His mule pulled up the stake pin one night and went into town dragging the rope and he followed as soon as daylight came. This was rather a dangerous undertaking but he said he was going to have his mule, Mexicans or no Mexicans. He pursued the runaway down the street until he caught hold of the rope, and then mounting, put back to camp quickly. A few Mexican women opened their doors on hearing the clatter of the mule's feet, but on seeing a dread Texan, shut them again quickly. The hour being so early the inhabitants were not astir.

The Texans stayed here a short time, but as no warlike demonstrations were made by the citizens, the command went back to the Texas side of the river. General Somervell had made a requisition on the town for 100 head of horses, but as they were not supplied, Jack Hays was sent with 70 men to demand $5000 in lieu of the horses. The Alcalde came into the Texans' camp with $700, declaring it was all that could be raised, and that the horses could not be procured, as they had been driven off by the rancheros, who had retreated from the town on the appearance of the Texans.

There were some hard feelings on the part of some of the men against Somervell, so about the 9th of December, he determined to abandon the expedition and gave orders for the troops to march to Gonzales and there be disbanded. When this order was given, five of the captains, with most of their men, refused to comply. These captains were William S. Fisher, Ewen Cameron, Eastland, Reese and Pierson. Captain Hays returned with the Somervell party, but some of his company, among whom was Wallace, remained with those who still had an idea of invading Mexico. They said that they did not come out there to rob houses and women, but to fight Mexicans and they were going to do it before they returned. Wallace says they had enough men then to capture Matamoros.

Officers and privates from other companies came over to them until the force numbered about 300. About 200 men went back and arrived at San Antonio about the last of January, 1843.

The companies under the five captains who had separated themselves from the balance of the command, marched down the river four miles and encamped for the night. The next day they elected Captain Fisher to the command and continued their march down the river. On the 21st they encamped opposite the town of Mier. What an ominous name! How the hearts of the readers of Texas history now thrill at the mention of it, although at that time having no significance.

The town of Mier was six miles from the camp of the Texans. On the following morning they crossed the Rio Grande, marched to the town, and made a requisition on the Alcalde for provisions and clothing. He promised that the articles should be delivered the next day at the river, but below the Texans' camp. The Texans, when they went back to their camp, brought the Alcalde along with them as surety for the delivery of the goods. On the 23rd the Texans moved their camp opposite the place where the goods were to be delivered, but the day passed off, and the next, and still the goods did not come. The Texas spies, who had been kept on the west side of the river, on the morning of the 24th captured a Mexican, who reported that General Ampudia had arrived at Mier with troops and prevented the fulfillment of the Alcalde's promise. The Texans then determined to again cross the river and give them battle. By 4 o'clock in the evening they had all crossed and were on their march to the town. Captain Baker had command of the spies and first met the Mexicans who sallied out from Mier. Ampudia retreated before the Texans and at dark again entered the town.

The Texans advanced to the Alcantra Creek east of the town. They halted for some time as this little stream ran very rapidly and it was difficult to find a crossing in the night, but finally succeeded in getting over. By this time a lively fight had commenced between Baker's spies and the Mexican cavalry and five of the Texans had been cut off and captured. Among these were Dr. Sinnickson, Sam Walker, Beasly and "Legs" Lewis. Others made narrow escapes. It was a hand-to-hand fight and the Texans who were cut off were compelled to abandon their horses and take across fences and ditches. Sam Walker was caught by a powerful Mexican and held down while others tied him. One man named McMullins was caught by the legs while getting over a fence, but his boots pulled off and he made his escape. Wallace was in town, or the edge of it rather, and told the men they would be caught, as he saw the Mexican cavalry and was getting back himself. He passed "Legs" Lewis and said: "The Mexicans will get you. You had better run." After the main body of the Texans had crossed the creek, they advanced to the town and passed down a street leading to the public square where the Mexicans had planted their artillery. While going into the town the Texans were fired on and a man named Jones was killed. He was the next man in the rear of Wallace as they galloped in single file and "Bigfoot" felt the wind of the bullet that killed Jones. Captain Wallace says that he was a well-dressed man and his impression was that he was once Postmaster General. The Mexicans attempted to strip his body and a lively fight ensued in which twenty of them were killed. When the Texans got near the cannon, they were halted by a terrible discharge of grape shot which swept the streets and caused them to seek shelter behind the buildings. It was now dark, Christmas evening, 1842. The only chance for the Texans to advance was by opening passage ways through the buildings and advance by degrees towards the cannon.

CHAPTER XII

BATTLE OF MIER.

It was dark when the Texans entered the town of Mier and most of them left their horses in camp under a guard and came in on foot. When they took possession of the buildings to avoid the discharge from the cannon, they at once commenced opening passage ways from house to house, fighting as they went, and by daylight arrived within fifty yards of the guns. While engaged in this work, Wallace found a Mexican baby which had been abandoned during the hasty exit of the occupants of the houses at the commencement of the fight. It set up a terrible squalling. "Bigfoot" took it up, advanced to a wall enclosing the yard, climbed up, and dropped it down on the other side, at the same time shouting out in Spanish for someone to come and get the muchacho. He soon heard a woman's voice on the outside and he supposed it was taken care of.

At daylight port holes were opened and the deadly crack of the rifle commenced on the artillerymen. The cannons were soon silenced for it was death for a Mexican to attempt to go near them. During the day three desperate attempts were made by the enemy to storm and carry the position of the Texans, but all failed with fearful loss. Wallace says they came so thick it was impossible to miss them, and the bravest of them was the Presidioales (town guards) who wore black hats with white bands around them, and who were nearly all killed. In one of the rooms occupied by the Texans, and where Wallace was, a strong Mexican drink called "aguardiente" was found and the men at once commenced drinking it to excess. Even one of their officers drank so much that he fell on the floor and was wounded by a bullet which came through a crack. The men were so worn out from their night's work that when they found this liquor they drank it out of tin cups like water. Bigfoot seeing it would render them unfit for service, turned the balance of the fire water out on the floor.

Before the fight commenced, Wallace says one of their scouts named Joe Berry fell down a bluff and broke his leg. His brother Bates and some others who were with him carried Joe to an out-building and placed him there. They were found out during the battle and their position attacked by the Mexicans. A sally was made in an attempt to reach the position of their companions but none arrived there except Berry. Austin, a bugler who was one of the party, was killed. Lieutenant Algerette, the Mexican officer who was in command of the party who assailed the position of the wounded Berry, went in and killed him with a sword as he lay helpless. He then bragged about it after the surrender and exhibited the sword which still had the blood of the gallant young Texan upon it.

During the fight in the night bugles were constantly sounding and it was reported that the Mexicans were being largely reinforced. The Texans were undismayed and continued to load their rifles and fire with such deadly effect that great confusion reigned among the Mexicans who continually uttered cries of rage and pain amid a constant blast of bugles. After it was no longer possible for the Mexicans to go near the cannon and their charges had been repulsed, they occupied the house tops and other places convenient to shoot from. They kept their bodies hid as much as possible and many of those killed were shot in the head. Wallace says he loaded and fired his rifle fifteen times, and that he always waited for a good chance, and had a bead on a Mexican every time he touched the trigger. The Mexicans tried to recover the cannons by throwing ropes around them from the corners of the buildings and succeeded in bringing some of them away.

During the fight after daylight on the 26th, the small guard which had been left on the east side of Alcantra Creek attacked about 60 of the Mexican cavalry and routed them, but perceiving a large body of the enemy coming to assail them, they decided to make a desperate attempt to join their comrades in the town. With this determination they made a charge into the ranks of the Mexicans and at the same time firing with fatal effect, but the odds were too great. Out of the nine men who made the attempt, only two of them succeeded in reaching their companions. Four were killed and three captured.

During one close charge of the Mexicans many were killed and wounded on both sides. Among the wounded were Colonel Fisher. Captain Cameron had fortified himself and men in the rear of the building occupied by Fisher and had been exposed to a fearful fire during which he had three men killed and seven wounded. The bugles of the Mexicans began sounding a charge from different parts of the town and Cameron hastily entered the room occupied by Fisher and his men and asked for a reinforcement to help defend the position. About that time a white flag was brought out by Dr. Sinnickson, one of the men who had been captured. He was ordered to do so by General Ampudia and to tell the Texans he had 1700 troops in the city and 300 more on the road from Monterrey, and that it would be useless for them to continue to resist, and that if they would surrender they would be treated as prisoners of war; if not, no quarter would be given. The prospect was gloomy for the Texans. Although they had fought as men worthy of the name Texans and had caused the streets of Mier to almost run with Mexican blood, they still saw no chance to conquer. They were on foreign soil, hemmed in on all sides by their enemies, their number reduced, and their survivors almost worn out. Still, some of them were opposed to a surrender and thought they could fight their way back across the Rio Grande. Many among Fisher's men, however, were in favor of a surrender. Cameron, who was opposed to it, hurried back to his men to exhort them to continue the fight. Others under the different captains favored a surrender and commenced leaving their positions and giving up their arms in the streets. When Fisher's men commenced going out to surrender, whom Wallace had been with part of the time, he left them and ran to the position of Cameron. Others now left their commands and came to Cameron until forty of them stood by him, asking him to take command and continue the battle, or make a sally and cut their way out. At this time great confusion prevailed; some of the men were surrendering, while others were preparing to continue the fight. Every few minutes barricades would be torn away and men would march out, four or five at a time, and surrender. Cameron held his position with the forty men who had rallied to him until all the balance had surrendered. Seeing that all hope was gone, he said to his men, who with stern, but anxious faces stood around him, "Boys, it is no use to continue to fight any longer. They are all gone but us and we will have to knock under." The men stood in silence for a moment and looked sternly at the hordes of Mexicans who were now making a grand display, cavalry cavorting in the streets and others carrying away the guns of the Texans, who were

now prisoners and bunched together on the plaza. The Mexican soldiers and the citizens of the town were making a great outcry and cheering for victory. A gallant officer named Thomas J. Green, who was with Cameron, broke his sword before he would give it up. Wallace was bitterly opposed to a surrender. He remembered the fate of his brother and cousin after they surrendered at Goliad and expected nothing else for himself and comrades on this occasion, and told them so. The gallant Cameron wished to save the lives of his men and taking the lead, they followed. They were met by a strong detachment of Mexicans as they emerged from their position into the street and the painful work of handing over their guns, pistols and knives commenced. Wallace stayed back to the last, closely watching every incident of the surrender, thinking likely it might be necessary to kill another Mexican if the slaughter he expected would follow, commenced prematurely. He at last handed up his arms and was the last man to do so at Mier. He says that as they were being marched to the square, his shoes became red with blood where the Mexicans bled who were killed during those desperate charges. He also saw blood in the gutters and on the housetops where they had bled. He says a Mexican whom General Somervell raised and educated was killed in the fight on the Mexican side and that he had Somervell's rifle with him.

The Mexican loss in the battle was fearful considering the numbers engaged, which was 2000 on the Mexican side, 500 of whom were killed, according to their own report of the battle. The Texans had 260 men, sixteen of whom were killed and thirty wounded. The Mexicans had forty artillerymen killed before they would give up trying to work their guns which were in close rifle shot of the place where the Texans were posted.

Captain Wallace says he thinks there were more than 800 Mexicans killed, and while the results were not so great, it was a harder fought battle than that of San Jacinto. He says that they were carried up to the square. From where the surrender took place, he saw four rows of dead Mexicans lying close together, reaching across the plaza, and that the priests were among them saying mass.

While this was being done, the bodies of the slain Texans, stripped of their clothing, were being dragged through the streets by the cavalry, followed by crowds of yelling Mexicans of all sizes and ages.

CHAPTER XIII

THE CAPTIVE TEXANS - FIGHT AT SALADO - ESCAPE OF THE PRISONERS

On the last days of December, General Ampudia set out with his prisoners for the City of Mexico, leaving the wounded at Mier under the care of Dr. Sinnickson. On January 9, 1843, the captive Texans arrived at Matamoros and on the 14th set out from that place, guarded by a troop of cavalry, and arrived in Monterrey on the 28th, where they remained until February 20. On the march to Monterrey it was one continual jubilee with the Mexicans. They starved the prisoners and made them go on foot all the way until they were almost barefoot and haggard. The Mexicans made grand demonstrations in passing through towns, their approach being heralded with bugle blasts and prancing, charging cavalry. The Texans were marched through the principal streets, followed by yelling mobs of men and boys. The women, however, with but few exceptions pitied the half-starved and half-dead Americans, some of whom were beardless boys, and when they arrived in Monterrey, the women came out with provisions and fed the Americans.

From Monterrey the prisoners were carried to Saltillo where they found six of the Texans who were captured at San Antonio the year before when General Woll visited the place. Bigfoot Wallace was still wearing the pants of the Mexican whom he killed at the battle of Salado.

At Saltillo Colonel Barragan took charge of the prisoners and proceeded with them to the Hacienda Salado, 100 miles further on. There they arrived on the 10th and were placed in prison. For some times past, the Texans had contemplated making an attempt to escape and had formulated the plan at Monterrey, but one of their own officers disclosed the plot to the Mexicans and the attempt was not made. Now it was set on foot again without detection and carried out. There had been an addition to their number of a portion of the Santa Fe prisoners who had gone on the ill-starred expedition to New Mexico. They had all been captured and sent over into Old Mexico and confined with the Mier prisoners; also, a few survivors of Dawson's Massacre had been placed with them. Among the Santa Fe prisoners were Drs. Brennan and Lyons who were anxious to make the attempt to escape. When all was ready Captain Cameron gave the signal by throwing up his hat and Lyons and Brennan led the charge on the guards. Cameron and Samuel H. Walker, who was captured before the battle of Mier, each charged a guard and succeeded in disarming them. This was at sunrise on the 11th day of February, 1843.

As soon as the first charge was made and the guards were disarmed at the door of the prison, the Texans rushed into the outer court of the building where there were 150 infantry guarding the arms and cartridge boxes. There were about 200 Texans and without hesitating an instant, rushed upon the Mexican soldiers with their naked hands. A desperate struggle commenced for the possession of the guns and cartridges. The Mexicans who were stationed inside the court of the prison fired hastily and surrendered, or fled.

The Texans were not yet masters of the situation as there was another company of infantry stationed at the gate and a force of cavalry also had formed outside to cut off their escape. Without waiting, the desperate men rushed upon these and a terrible fight ensued. Most of the Texans had secured guns when the second hand-to-hand encounter occurred. Bigfoot had secured no gun as yet and rushed upon a Mexican to disarm him, but the fellow had a bayonet on the gun and made a desperate thrust at the big Texan. Wallace seized the bayonet and a hard struggle commenced for the mastery, but the bayonet soon came off in Wallace's hands. Another disarmed prisoner came up behind and seized the breach and got possession of the gun, which, however, had no load in it as the soldier had just fired it.

The fight at this time was fiercely raging and Wallace went into it brandishing the bayonet which he used until the fight was over. In vain the Mexicans tried to keep the Texans from going through the gate which would give them their liberty. The contest was short, but bloody, and the noise and confusion was awful. The Mexicans uttered yells and screams of terror and surprise as the Texans rushed among them with clubbed guns after the first discharge and delivered blows right and left. The cavalry became terror stricken and fled. The infantry began to throw down their arms and tried to surrender, but for a time no stop could be put to the slaughter. At length the voice of Cameron was heard who went among the men and begged for the lives of the disarmed guards. Wallace says they ceased to kill any more of them, but would strike them on the head occasionally when they moved to make them stand still. Many Mexicans lay dead on every side, while others were moaning with broken heads and gunshot wounds. One Mexican lieutenant, Barragan, son of the commander, displayed great bravery during the fight. Drawing his sword, he backed against a wall and successfully parried five or six bayonet thrusts. Someone suggested to Wallace to get a loaded gun and shoot him, but Wallace said no, that a brave man like him should be spared. The young officer was then called on to surrender and hand over his sword, but he refused, saying he would not surrender his sword to a private but would give up to Captain Cameron. This officer was called and the Lieutenant at once surrendered his sword. His father, Colonel Barragan, had quit the field in ignominious flight. Other Mexicans who had surrendered and were looking on during this episode said this Lieutenant did not derive his courage from his father, but from his mother, and that he favored her.

The Texans did not come out of the fight unscratched. Five of their comrades lay still and motionless among their dead foes, and many were wounded and unable to rise from the ground. Among the killed were the brave and fearless Brennan and Lyons who led the attack at the prison door. The Texans being masters of the situation, dictated terms to the Mexicans, one of which was that their wounded should be taken care of. Those who were able to travel prepared for instant flight, for they knew this was their only chance for safety, as a large force would soon be on their trail.

Some of the Mexican cavalry, who tied their horses, and were not close to them when the onset was made, ran away without mounting. Other horses were found in the town and soon enough were secured to mount the men. By 10 o'clock in the forenoon they set out for the Rio Grande. Bigfoot Wallace secured a fine dun pacing mule which belonged to Captain Arroyo, who had run away and left the mule. By midnight they went fifty miles, made a short halt, fed their horses, then went twelve miles further, and again halting, slept two hours. Early next morning they left the main road in order to go around the city of Saltillo. On the

13th they struck the road leading from Saltillo to Monclova, but on the next night abandoned it, and took to the mountains on the left. This was a fatal mistake as events which follow will show.

The trouble and hardships of these brave men now commenced in earnest. When too late they saw the mistake which they had made. The country was a barren waste of mountains, without water or anything in the shape of food. Six days were spent in trying to get through. The men were perishing with thirst and starvation. Horses were killed and eaten and their blood drank by the desperate Texans. Bigfoot Wallace killed the fine dun mule of Captain Arroyo. He and others of his comrades ravenously devoured quantities of it and quaffed cups-full of the red blood with gusto and apparent relish as if they were drinking to one anothers health in the saloons of San Antonio.

Sitting around our firesides at home, surrounded by our families and home comforts, we can hardly realize the gravity or horribleness of the situation in the dry lonely canyon, where the horses were killed to sustain human life. The bloody feast akin to savage orgies can only be understood rightly by those who participated in it. They could not long remain here, swarms of cavalrymen with pack mules carrying provisions and water were on their trail. Leaving the remains of the slaughtered horses for the coyotes to finish, the Texans once more plunged into the dark mountains in a vain effort to reach the Rio Grande. They were hopelessly lost, and once more they began to suffer with thirst. They could no longer keep together as a body. The horses which had not been killed for food were dead or abandoned. Men became delirious and, wandering away, died alone in the dry, hot ravines or on top of lofty mountains amid huge rocks. They could no longer carry their guns, and they were thrown away, at least most of them, and they toiled on. Men would sink down with their heads dropped on their breasts and their feet pointing in the direction they wished to go. Bigfoot Wallace had partly dried some of his mule meat in the hot sun and was carrying it in a haversack. He would from time to time partake of the meat until his thirst became so intense he could no longer do so. His tongue was dry and useless, swelled to the roof of his mouth. Five more days he spent without water, but during that time his legs never failed him. The men now were badly scattered. Wallace and three companions stayed together and toiled on with faces turned in the direction they thought the Rio Grande to be.

CHAPTER XIV

RECAPTURED BY THE MEXICANS - MARCHED BACK TO SALADO

The Mexican cavalry who were on the trail of the fugitive Texans, finally began to come upon those who were behind and captured them. Then they came up with the main body who had remained together. Some of them carried their guns and although emaciated and nearly famished until they resembled dead men, refused to surrender except as prisoners of war. This was agreed to by the Mexicans and all were again taken. Wallace and his three companions, who were Captain Cameron, Tom Davis and James Ogden, were headed off and captured within one hundred and fifty yards of a pool of water. They thought from the looks of the country that water was near, and were using their last remaining strength to get to it. The Mexicans dealt out the water sparingly to the Texans, fearing they would kill themselves if allowed to drink all they wanted at once. While they were dispensing a small cupfull to each man, Wallace noticed a cavalryman near him who had the water gourd which had been taken from him at Mier. Thinking they would all be shot anyway and rendered desperate by the situation, Wallace sprang at him and said in Spanish, "That is my gourd, give it up." The Mexican soldier at once complied, saying: "Pobrecito" (poor fellow.) Wallace turned up the gourd and says that the first swallow was the best he ever tasted and continued to gurgle it down. Tom Davis ran up to him and said "give me some `foot.'" Wallace said he couldn't turn it loose and Davis was unable to pull the gourd from his mouth. A Mexican officer said "Hell" (in Spanish) "take the water away from that fellow, he will kill himself." Three or four soldiers then tried to take the gourd from the big Texan but was unable to do so until he had emptied it. After Bigfoot had drank the water, which was near a gallon, he turned and dropped down on his knapsack and said he never felt so good in his life and in an instant went to sleep. He had not slept any for five nights. When he fell down the officer said: "See, now he is dead." It seems that the officers who were in command of this squad were humane and treated these four prisoners well, even Captain Cameron. They camped here for the night so that the worn men could rest and occasionally through the night would give them a little more water. Wallace slept all night without moving and the soldiers thought he would not wake anymore but would die that way. When morning came Wallace roused up refreshed and hungry, and opening his knapsack, began to make a hearty meal of his remaining mule meat. Some of the Mexicans said "Look at that man, he is not dead, watch him eat." One of them came to him and asked what he was eating. "Mule meat" said Bigfoot, as he looked at the Mexican in the face. "Whose mule was it?" was the next question.

"My mule," says Wallace.

"It was not," said the Mexican. "He belonged to Captain Arroyo."

"Why didn't he stay with him then," said the Texan as he continued to eat. "He ran off and left him and I got him, so he belonged to me, and when I got hungry, I killed him and ate him. Mule meat is good, better than horse meat."

The Mexicans made diligent search and brought in all they could find in the mountains, but of the 193 who made their escape after the fight at the

Hacienda Salado, five died of thirst and starvation, four got through to Texas and three were never found or heard of.

Stragglers continued to be brought in and at first all were tied together with ropes and marched in long strings. On the 27th their number had increased to 160 and were then carried to Saltillo. An order came there from Santa Anna, for them to be shot. This the officer in command refused to do, saying he would resign his commission first. The British consul also interfered and had it stopped. One of the prisoners, James C. Wilson, was a British subject, and the consul proposed to set him at liberty, but he refused to accept it, saying he was a Texan and would die with his comrades if necessary. The prisoners were then all ironed and marched back to Salado, the scene of the fight, where they arrived on the 24th of March. Here another order came from Santa Anna that every 10th man should be shot. The irons were kept on the prisoners and double guards put around them. When the prisoners arrived at the scene of their break for liberty, Bigfoot and Henry Whaling were near to each other and noticed some Mexicans were digging a ditch. Whaling remarked: "That ditch is for us." These were prophetic words so far as Whaling was concerned, for he drew a black bean, was shot, and put into the ditch along with his unfortunate companions who also drew the fatal beans.

CHAPTER XV

DRAWING THE BEANS FOR LIFE.

In decimating the prisoners, it was decided by the Mexicans to let them draw lots and each man have a chance for his life. The lots were to be determined by drawing beans. The white beans meaning life, and the black beans meaning death. A pitcher was procured and ten white beans to one black one were placed in it.

When all was ready, the Texans were marched out a short distance and formed in line. An officer came up bearing the fatal pitcher in which there were 159 white beans and 17 black ones. Few men, even in regular wartime, pass through such a fearful ordeal as the men did who drew beans for their lives at Salado.

For a few moments the men stood in silence and then the drawing commenced. No severer test could have been made of men's nerve than on this occasion. They will rush almost to certain death in the excitement of battle, but to stand and decide their fate in a second by the drawing of a bean, was worse than charging into the muzzle of a blazing cannon. The Mexicans were very anxious to kill Captain Cameron and were in hopes he would draw a black bean so they would have some excuse to shoot him. The black beans were placed on top and Cameron was made to draw first. As he reached for the pitcher which was held high so no one could see into it, one of the captives, William F. Wilson, said: "Dip deep Captain." He did so and pulled out a white bean and then stepped back into

line. A look of satisfaction passed over the faces of the Texans, for they all loved the brave and unselfish Cameron, but the Mexicans scowled. The drawing went on rapidly, only a few hesitating to pull forth their bean in this terrible game of life. When the time came for Wallace to draw, he stepped up quietly and reached for the pitcher, but his hand was so large he had some difficulty and had to squeeze his hand down to the beans.

Wallace was among the last to draw which made his chance less, as the boys had dipped deep until there were nearly as many black beans as there were white ones. He had to scoop beans with two fingers on account of their scarcity and the crowded position of his hand. He succeeded in getting up two and held them a few moments feeling of them. The Mexicans were watching closely and an officer said to Wallace: "Don't you pull out two. If you do, and one of them is black, you will have to take it." Bigfoot paid no attention to him, but felt of the beans until he discovered that one was a little larger than the other. He let the larger one drop and pulled forth his hand. Between his fingers he held a white bean. He is satisfied that the one he dropped was black. The next two men to draw were Wing and Whaling; both drew black beans.

The last three men on the list did not draw, as the 17 black beans were all taken out. An officer turned up the pitcher or jar and three white beans fell to the ground. Wallace says the vessel they drew the beans from was not a pitcher, but a jar, and that it tapered both ways something like a ten pin. When Wallace drew his hand out of the vessel, a Mexican officer took hold of it to examine it and called up others to see how large it was. The prisoners were chained together, two and two, and drew their beans in alphabetical order. The man to whom Wallace was chained was named Sensubaugh and had to draw before his companion. Captain Wallace says if there ever was a Christian, it was this man. He prayed for himself and Bigfoot that they might be spared. He drew a white bean and afterwards amid clanking chains in the dark dungeon of Perote, prayed and sang hymns, and thanked God that it was as well with him as it was.

Although the men knew that some were compelled to draw black beans, they could not help showing looks of satisfaction as friend after friend drew those beans which gave them life. What keen pangs, however, of sorrow and regret shot through their hearts when the fatal black beans came forth, held by some dear friend or comrade who had stood by them during all the fearful hardships and dangers through which they had passed, but were now compelled to die - shot like a dog, far from home and loved ones. Most of the men showed the utmost coolness, scarcely a tremor passing over their faces as the drawing progressed. One noted gambler, when his time came to draw, stepped up with a smile and said: "Boys, this is the highest stake I ever played for." When he drew forth his hand his fingers held a black bean and without changing the smile on his face, took his place in the death line and remarked, "Just my luck."

As fast as the black beans were drawn out, the unfortunate holder was placed in the death line. Sometimes the two chained together would draw black beans and would not have to be separated, but moved together to the fatal line. When one was taken and the other left, the chains were taken off and the condemned coupled to one of his companions in distress. Young Robert Beard was very sick and had to be held up to draw his bean. Before drawing, he requested of his brother that if he drew a black bean and himself a white one, to exchange with him, and he would die in his place, and the well one might live to get back home. His brother would not agree to this but they both drew white beans and lived to return home.

It is generally believed and told that Bigfoot Wallace drew two beans at Salado; that one of his comrades, a young fellow bewailed his situation, and expressed his fear that he would draw a black bean in such a way, that Wallace told him to hush and take his bean he had just drawn and that he would take another chance. When the writer asked Captain Wallace in regard to this he said: "No, I never drew but one and was terribly glad when I saw that it was white and had no idea of giving it away." He says this tale likely grew out of the episode of the Beard brothers. And another thing he said they could not have done so if they wished, for he heard an officer say that there should be no swapping of beans. M. C. Wing, a young man, was the last man on the list to draw a black bean and was perceptibly affected. He had been very religious when at home, but had left the beaten track of christianity and gone sadly astray, and that seemed to trouble him a great deal.

One young fellow, a mere boy, drew a black bean, and giving one appealing look at his comrades, asked them to avenge his death.

"Talking" Bill Moore, when it came his turn to draw said: "Boys, I had rather draw for a Spanish horse and lose him." He was a lively fellow and helped to keep up the spirits of the balance. Good fortune favored him and he drew a white bean. When the drawing was over and the condemned men stood in the death rank chained two and two together, their roll stood as follows: L. L. Cash, J. D. Cocke, Robert Durham, William N. Eastland, Edward Este, Robert Harris, S. L. Jones, Patrick Mahan, James Ogden, Charles Roberts, William Rowan, J. L. Shepard (cousin of the writer), J. M.

N. Thompson, James N. Torry, James Turnbull, Henry Whaling and M. C. Wing.

Henry Whaling then asked for something to eat, saying, "I do not want to starve and be shot too." Strange to say the Mexicans complied with the request and issued him two soldiers' rations which he ate. While the drawing was in progress some of the petty Mexican officers did everything in their power to annoy and tantalize the wretched men. When one drew a black bean they would express great sorrow and tell him to cheer up, better luck next time, when they knew this was his last chance. When all was over the men stood in silence, not a sound was heard among them. Those in the death line intently watched their captors. When the firing squad was detailed and counted off, some little sign of emotion was visible in the countenances of a few who were to be executed and so soon to face the deadly muskets. Their bosoms heaved and the breath came short and quick. Others stood calm as if on parade.

The irons were taken off of them and they were led away to execution, bidding their comrades farewell as they marched off. Many tears were seen running down the emaciated and sunburned faces of their more fortunate companions as they responded to this last goodbye.

When they arrived at the place of execution, the Texans asked permission to be shot in front, but were refused. Henry Whaling tried to get them not to blindfold him, saying he wanted to look at the man who shot him and show them how a Texan could die. This, however, was refused. The Mexicans stood close to their backs when they fired, and all fell to the ground. The soldiers then stripped them and piled up their bodies like cordwood. They were all dead but one, J. L. Shepard. He was only wounded in the shoulder, but went through the process of being stripped and piled up without showing any signs of life. When the soldiers left he made his escape to the mountains. There he remained ten days suffering with hunger and his festering wound, but was again captured, brought back and executed.

Some say that James C. Wilson, the English subject, made his escape before the drawing of the beans, but Captain Wallace says it was after. No doubt the British consul interfered to liberate him but he would not accept it. He lived to return to Texas and lived many years honored and respected. He died in Gonzales county. Wilson county was named for him. His son, Judge James C. Wilson, lives in Karnes County and is district judge.

CHAPTER XVI

MARCHED TO THE CITY OF MEXICO.

After the execution of the unfortunate Texans, the survivors were started out heavily ironed for the City of Mexico. All that were able had to walk and it is impossible to describe what they suffered. They were carried through all the principal cities on the route, driven like so many cattle, and almost starved. They were derided, hooted at and maltreated all the way by the populace.

The shackles on Bigfoot Wallace were too small and cut deep into the flesh. His arms swelled and turned black. When they arrived at San Luis Potosi the governor's wife came to look at the prisoners and noticed the condition of Wallace. Her woman's sympathies were at once aroused and she ordered the chains to be taken off. The officer in command refused to do this, saying only the governor had authority to give such an order. She replied to this that she was the governor's wife and ordered him again to take them off. This time he complied and sent for a blacksmith who removed them. The good woman then bathed the black and swollen arms with brandy with her own hands. Seeing others of the prisoners suffering also who had gathered around, she ordered the blacksmith to take the chains off of all of them. Before she did this, however, she asked the officer in command if he was afraid of his prisoners without chains on and he said "No!" When all this was accomplished, Wallace told her she ought to be president of Mexico.

On the march to the capital, after the chains had been taken off, Bigfoot made good use of his long arms as he passed through the towns. He would reach and get cakes and tamales off the stands of vendors of these things. The owners would make great outcry but the Mexican soldiers only laughed. Sometimes they would meet one carrying a tray or board of good things on his head, but Wallace was so much taller than the little squatty Mexican that he could reach down and get a handfull of things without the owner knowing it. Bigfoot with his gaunt form and long arms was a great curiosity to them. He could pass one of those stands and then reach back and get the article from it.

When they arrived at a little Indian village 18 miles from the City of Mexico, an order came from Santa Anna to shoot Captain Ewen Cameron. This was kept secret from the balance of the prisoners for fear they would make an outbreak. They took Cameron that night and put him in a room alone and the balance of the men were huddled together in a small cell where they almost suffocated. They had suspicion, however, from their transactions that Cameron was to be shot. The next morning when they were all marched out to a tank to wash, each man filled his bosom full of rocks, determined to fight for their beloved captain and die with him if an attempt was made on his life. The guards asked why they were getting the rocks and they were told it was for ballast so they could walk better. They made no attempt to take them away - in fact they were afraid to as they could see the men looked desperate. The march was at once taken up early in the morning. The prisoners asked about their captain and if he were to be killed, but the Mexicans said no and for them to go, that he would come on soon. When the prisoners got one mile from the place on rising ground they heard a platoon of gunfire back at the town and they knew that the gallant Cameron had met his fate.

It was a refinement of cruelty on the part of Santa Anna to have Cameron executed after he had drawn a white bean. He met his fate unflinchingly and died as none but the brave can die.

Before arriving at the capital the captives were again put in irons and convict garb placed upon them. In this condition and with grand display they were marched into the historic city of the Montezumas.

Before leaving San Antonio, Wallace had some shirts made which came down nearly to his ankles and when he wore his pants out until little more than the waistband was left, the Mexicans thought he was a priest and occasionally along the route before donning the convict suit, some of them would call him Padre and run out and give him a piece of tortilla. It was dry and hard but Wallace would soon mash it up between his teeth and relish it.

While being conveyed up the streets of the capital, the populace were unusually noisy, hooting, yelling and offering many insults. One old woman (squaw, Wallace called her) singled him out for her especial taunts and jeers. She was very ugly with a long grizzled neck and would come in front of him, grin and make all kinds of faces. The shackled Texan was almost desperate with the smarting of his chains and would have struck her if his hands had been loose, but as this was out of the question, he watched his chance. When her back was turned, he sprang at her and caught the back of her neck with his teeth thinking he would bite a piece out, but the old woman squalled like a panther and jerked loose. Bigfoot says that was the toughest meat he ever tried to bite. He could make no impression on it and his teeth slipped off and popped like a horse pulling his foot out of a bog. The soldiers laughed very heartily at this, ridiculed the old woman and bravoed the tall Gringo.

The British consul had a good deal to say about the killing of Cameron and talked to Santa Anna face-to-face, bitterly condemning his action.

It must be remembered that Texas did not belong to the United States at that time and was a republic. The United States had nothing to do in regard to protecting citizens of Texas and the new republic was not able to invade Mexico and release her citizens.

CHAPTER XVII

WORKING THE CAPTIVES.

The Texas prisoners arrived in the city of Mexico on the 1st day of May and remained there until the following October. During this time they were confined and closely guarded at night and worked with chains on during the day. Part of their work was to carry sand in sacks to make a fine road up to the Bishop's Palace where Santa Anna lived. The work was slow and tedious walking the lock step with chains around their ankles. Even at this, however, the Texans played off a good deal by punching their sacks full of holes and letting sand run out as they went along so that when they arrived at the dumping ground the load had become very light. Part of the time the prisoners worked at Molino del Rey, one and a half miles from the city, and here four prisoners escaped by scaling a wall. They were Samuel H. Walker, James C. Wilson and one Thompson and Gatis. It was late in the evening just before sundown and all the prisoners had been brought in for the night and placed in different rooms, but all surrounded by a wall. Before the regular guard was put on for the night (which was always doubled) the four men above mentioned scaled the wall while the sentinel's back was turned.

The man Thompson had played off on the march by wrapping bloody rags which he had secured some way, around his foot and leg, limping and making the most terrible faces. The Mexicans let him ride all the way and he had not been able to work much on account of the leg; falling and tumbling about every time he tried to walk. The men all knew Thompson was putting on and that there was nothing the matter with his leg. Wallace said he had rather walk or work than to make the faces and distortions that Thompson went through. When the sentinel came into the room where he had left the prisoners a few moments before and found it empty, the truth flashed across his mind at once, and bringing the butt of his gun down on the floor with considerable force, exclaimed "Caraja." He, however, did not report the loss and it was not found out until next morning. Then no one knew how it occurred. What mostly surprised the Mexicans was that the crippled man who got away had scaled a wall when they they did not think he was able to step over a rock a foot high. The four all made their way back to Texas. In October the prisoners were sent to Perote, distant about 300 miles from the capital. They had to walk all the way, but without chains on. Here they were confined in the damp, loathsome dungeon of Perote and the air was so bad that forty of them died. Wallace, with ten others, went wild and had to be tied down. All died but Wallace and he was tied down fourteen days. The Mexican doctors who were in attendance had their assistants rub Bigfoot to bring back circulation. In doing so, one of them pulled a plaster off his sore back and he knocked the Mexican who did it clear across the room.

Seeing they would all die if too closely confined, they were carried out to work during the day — Wallace with the balance as soon as he was able. They were hitched twenty-five to a cart and made to haul rocks from the mountains down to town. During this time the Texans let three carts accidently get the start of them, run off a high bluff and smash to pieces. They hitched Wallace to a cart alone on one occasion to haul some sand. A spirit of devilment coming over him, he pretended to get scared at something, ran away and could not be stopped until he had demolished the cart. It was a funny sight to the Mexicans to see a man running away with a cart and could not be stopped or headed off until it was overturned. They gave way to loud peals of laughter.

During this long confinement one of Jack Hays' old rangers named Joe Davis conceived the idea of digging under the dungeon wall which was five feet in thickness and twenty-two feet to get under the foundation. There were twenty-seven men confined in this apartment and all agreed to the plan and they went to work, digging at night and hiding their dirt as best they could. Some of the dirt was carried out in their clothing as they went to work on the streets and scattered gradually so as to escape detection. In this way they succeeded in digging under and out. This made a hole of forty-four feet they had to dig to get under and out, but they did it and twenty-four of them succeeded in getting clear. The plot was discovered soon after they got through. Wallace heard the men were all getting out of that room and he went there to get through also but found the room full of Mexican officers and soldiers and had to give it up. Four of those who got out were recaptured and brought back and chains put on all again. They were compelled to work hard and nearly starved. Many weary nights passed away and clanking chains could be heard at all hours. Many rats invaded the prison den and so near starved were the men that the rats were caught and eaten. The rats would run up the wall to the little cross-barred window where the sentinel stood, and going through, would drop into the dungeon. When the rat was heard to hit the floor, there would be a lively rattling of chains as each man tried to catch him. Captain Wallace says they were looked upon as an extra dish. When several could be secured they would save them for Sunday and have the cook make a pot of soup which was greatly enjoyed by the prisoners.

The captain in command here was a wooden-legged fellow with a long Mexican name which the Texans could not pronounce easy. The more irreverent ones of them called him "Limping Jesus." He would come in to inspect the cells with a great splutter of official dignity. One of the men drew a perfect picture of him on the wall which made him very angry and he had it defaced.

CHAPTER XVIII

RELEASED FROM PRISON.

If all the minute particulars were written of the interesting incidents through which the captive Texans passed, they would fill a large volume. The main points have been given, and enough of the minor details, to give the reader a clear conception of the situation. The pathetic incidents were occasionally interspersed with the ludicrous, which broke the monotony of prison life and suffering.

On one occasion while Bigfoot was crazed, and fighting and trying to tear everything in his reach, two young Mexican women of the higher or wealthy class expressed a great desire to see the wild Texan. They made known their wish to the Padre of the city and he promised to go with them to the prison. When they arrived at the entrance and the guards threw back the prison door, the dusky damsels drew back alarmed when they heard the clanking chains of the prisoners. The good father assured them, however, that there was no danger, that trusty guards were at hand, and the "Mucho Grande Loco Americano" was unusually docile. In the meantime some of the Texans who had seen the party enter and caught onto the import of their visit, went and informed Wallace who was lying on a cot. He at once raised up to a sitting position with his feet on the floor and completely enveloped himself in a sheet except for his eyes, and looked as much like a ghost as possible. When the party came up in front of Wallace and the shy

maidens were tremblingly viewing "El Loco hombre," (the mad man), Bigfoot threw off his sheet and uttering a yell that would have made a Comanche Indian turn pale, sprang at them. With one long wailing scream of terror and despair, the two Mexican girls sank to the floor and Wallace caught one of them by the foot. Great excitement now prevailed. The guards rushed in and seized Wallace and tried to loosen his grip on the girl, but not being able to do so, dragged Wallace and the girl about over the cell in a vain endeavor to pull him loose. The girl still screamed and Bigfoot uttered growls and roars like a caged lion. The Mexican soldiers cursed and threatened to cut him loose with their sabres, while the priest hopped about and called on all the saints both small and great that were laid down in his catechism. To add to the excitement of the scene, the Texans were rattling their chains and with upraised manacled hands threatening the soldiers if they used their sabres on Wallace.

At last in sheer desperation the priest sprang upon Wallace himself and the tension on his muscles was so great as the soldiers continued to drag them about that he was compelled to turn loose. He was carried to his couch, while the girl fairly flew from the prison with her disheveled hair streaming behind her. The other girl had vamoosed. The priest went out with a quick step and flushed face.

During all these tedious months of captivity, friends in the United States were using their best endeavors to have the prisoners liberated. The young Republic of Texas was not able alone to send an invading army into Mexico and strike the chains from her citizens, but did all she could in conjunction with others to have it done by the Mexican authorities. The wife of Santa Anna, who was an invalid and a good woman, pleaded with the stern dictator for their release. He was greatly attached to her and would grant almost anything she asked.

Not long after this, four of the prisoners were released through the intervention of influential friends in the United States. These four were Bigfoot Wallace, Thomas Tatum, James Armstrong and William F. Wilson. Wallace was liberated through his father and Governor McDowell of Virginia. Their plantations joined and the two families were friends of long standing.

Thomas Tatum, who was a native of Tennessee, gained his liberty through the influence of General Jackson.

William F. Wilson, who was also a native of Virginia, was released through the influence of Governor McDowell.

The chains dropped from the manacled wrists of James Armstrong through the good offices of Thomas Benton of Missouri.

On the 5th day of August, 1844, the four men in question walked out from the dark Perote dungeon free men after a confinement of twenty-two months. On the same day the wife of Santa Anna died, loved and regretted by every Texan who wore the chains in Mexico.

As to the balance of the prisoners, suffice it to say that soon after the death of the president's wife, the president gave orders for all of the Texas prisoners to be liberated.

He had promised his wife on her deathbed that he would do so and let it go to Santa Anna's credit that once in life he kept his promise.

When Bigfoot and his three companions once more breathed free air they set out on foot in the hot, broiling sun for Vera Cruz. They had one dollar apiece which was given them by the prison officials to defray their expenses out of the country. On the route they passed through the city of

Jalapa, one of the cleanest and nicest, Wallace says he ever saw.

The Mexicans treated them kindly along the route when convinced that they were not French. One woman gave Wallace water and fanned him when he came to her door nearly dead with heat after a long tramp across a sandy plain.

Bigfoot says it is always spring in Jalapa and has the finest looking women in Mexico; all Castilians and not "Pumpkin-colored Mexicans," as he expressed it.

When they arrived at Vera Cruz the people were dying by the hundreds with yellow fever and they could not find a ship bound for New Orleans where they intended going. One ship had just left before they arrived. Eleven days they had to remain here and then had to board a condemned ship to get away. The vessel was bound for the dry dock at New Orleans and was commanded by a South Sea island captain. It had been a French merchant ship and was very large. The captain said if they were Mier prisoners he would not charge them anything.

By the time they got aboard and underway Wallace and his crowd and six sailors had the yellow fever. The old captain of the ship was not alarmed at this for he said he could cure them if they would take his medicine. His first treatment was an average bottle of castor oil which he required them to take at two doses a short time apart. His next was a bitter concoction made of red looking roots which he brought from the South sea islands. Captain Wallace says the roots looked like radishes. Before they arrived at New Orleans the sick men had all recovered and able to eat full rations.

Friends had deposited funds at New Orleans for Wallace and his companions to draw upon, and on this Wallace had contracted for their rations on board during the passage. A man named Young had charge of the commissary department and failed to issue them sailor's rations as per contract. This so enraged Wilson after they got so they could eat that he took hold of Young one morning and tried to throw him overboard and would have done so but for the intervention of Wallace. Wilson had Young nearly over when Wallace caught hold of him and pulled him back saying, "It will never do to be arrested for drowning such a damned rascal as he is." When the ship arrived at New Orleans, Young reported them as mutineers and tried hard to have the whole party arrested. When the authorities found out the nature of the case, they said the men ought to have sent him overboard. Wallace gave the captain an order on the prisoner's fund for their passage which he did not want to take, but Wallace insisted, and bidding him farewell, they separated in the streets of New Orleans.

Captain Wallace had an old schoolmate in the city named William Morehead, who was a lieutenant on the police force. Through him Wallace also obtained a position on the force. Bigfoot only served three weeks in this business, but in that time made $800 catching runaway negroes that rewards were offered for. He also had some stirring adventures. On one occasion a desperate sailor belonging to an English vessel was doing up the town and Wallace and Morehead were sent to arrest him. They soon found one man whose face was mashed into a pulp and the bloodiest man Wallace says he ever saw. When they came upon the belicose individual who was putting such ugly faces on people he squared himself for a fight and wanted to known their authority for demanding his surrender. For reply they showed him their clubs. The police clubs in those days were called colts and different to those now in use. They were heavily leaded and a more formidable weapon. The man went with them a short distance when they both took hold of him. Suddenly he struck Morehead a fearful blow on the right jaw and knocked him down. Before Wallace could do anything he received a lick which he partially dodged but which nearly tore his ear loose from the left side of his head. At the same time Wallace brought his club down with terrific force on the fellow's head which cut his cap in twain and brought him to the sidewalk. Bigfoot then reeled and fell himself from the effects of the blow which he had just received. This was all done in a few seconds and the trio were on the ground together. Morehead was the first to get up and planted his heels in the desperado's face. Wallace also got to his feet feeling pretty rickety, but laid hold of him and the two dragged the tough sailor about a block. Here they met a boy who said he was on the same ship with him and that the man was a deserter. In the office he made an attempt to escape, striking one man in the stomach, knocking him straight up in the air, and he came down on his head. Before the desperado could do anything more Wallace knocked him down with his club and he was dragged in and made fast in the stocks.

Morehead made a complaint for the lick struck him and wanted $75 damages. When Wallace was asked what he would put in for damages he said "nothing," and continued "If two big men like myself and Morehead cannot handle one man, I have no complaint to make." The old Captain still wears the sign of this lick.

Officers of the ship to which this fellow belonged were notified of his arrest and six marines armed with cutlasses were sent to bring him back to his vessel.

It was learned that this man had been a prize fighter and Wallace says he was the hardest fleshed man he ever had his hands on and his muscles were as hard as rocks.

Wallace says there was one clerk on the force named Everett who gave him an account one day of being cut by a man in the side with a pocket knife in 1837. Wallace knew he was the man who did it but said nothing.

CHAPTER XIX

RETURN TO TEXAS.

Bigfoot Wallace soon got tired of the city and once more craved to roam through the woods and over the prairies of Texas. Soon after the episode with the prize fighter, he left New Orleans and again took shipping for Galveston, Texas. He arrived without incident this time, but did not remain long, going from there to La Grange in an ox wagon. He was not satisfied to stay here and soon got in with a man named Carr who was going to carry a drove of cattle to San Antonio. The trip was made without incident and the cattle delivered on the river below town.

Wallace stayed in San Antonio awhile, met up with old friends and comrades, but finally decided to settle on the Medina River and farm some.

In 1845 Wallace erected his cabin on the banks of the Medina River and once more enjoyed the solitude of the great West.

Near Wallace's camp stood an old cannon carriage which had been abandoned by Santa Anna's army when they invaded Texas.

It was no trouble to get game as it was on every side. Deer, turkey, bear, panther, leopard and wildcat, and smaller game without end. Panthers were so numerous that he could not hang up a piece of meat outside of the cabin but they would get it. When Wallace would find a lot of young panthers he would take a club and kill them like kittens. If they were large enough to climb a tree, he would climb after them with a club and knock them out so the dogs could kill them. In one season there, he killed one hundred and forty-two of these animals up and down the Medina bottom. On one occasion he followed his dogs which were running a bear. On coming to them he saw that the bear was trying to climb a tree and one of the dogs was up on the side of the tree trying to pull the bear back. Wallace relieved him of the job by shooting bruin through the head.

Sometimes the Indians were friendly and at other times they were not. During their hostile season he had to be on the keen lookout. He was in danger all the time, living alone most of the time as he was.

On one occasion he was out on foot some distance from home and came upon a band of hostile Indians in a wooded country. The Indians were all on foot also, but at once gave chase. Wallace aimed his rifle and killed one and then fled. After running about three miles and leaving the Indians some distance behind, and his wind getting short, he entered a ravine and reloaded his rifle thinking there to make his stand and fight them, feeling he could run no further. The yells of the Indians, however, as they drew near put new life into him and leaving cover, he ran three more miles and escaped them.

Many sick men came from San Antonio to the camp of Wallace to eat wild roasted meat. Some got well, but others died who were too far gone to recover. One Lieutenant Casey of the army was brought out there in the last stages of consumption. When Wallace looked at him he told his friends who brought him that his case was hopeless, remarking "I can't bring the dead back to life." He died in a few days and his remains were sent back to New York. One Doctor Foster, however, who was so low and weak when he came that he could not talk above a whisper, recovered and left Wallace, fat and in good health and went to California.

At this time the Germans were settling at Castroville above Wallace's camp on the Medina, and Wallace was of great advantage to them as guide and trailer after hostile Indians who carried off their stock. The writer has been among those people a good deal collecting West Texas history, and the old fellows all have a good word to say about Bigfoot Wallace and tell many interesting incidents of their trips with him.

Mr. Peter Jungman, who now lives at Castroville, says that on one occasion himself, his brother John and some others were on a scout with Bigfoot. Night came on and they stopped to camp. It was in Indian times and no fire was made. When night closed down it had the appearance of rain and Wallace, approaching an overhanging rock near by, expressed his intention of sleeping there. Others said they would too and began to gather up their blankets, but about this time the warning sound of a rattlesnake was heard where they contemplated passing the night and all drew back except Wallace. He picked up a stick and said: "Old fellow, you have got to vacate, I'm going to sleep here," and with the stick thrashed him off into the brush telling him to "Git! git!!" with each blow. He then put his gun and blanket under, crawled under himself and went to sleep.

On another occasion a young man named Phil Hodges, who now lives in Sabinal Canyon, went out with Bigfoot to hunt horses. They carried no provisions along and hunted all day without dinner. At sundown they were eight miles from the ranch and young Hodges was terribly hungry and thinking how long it would be yet before they could get anything, when Wallace stopped his horse under a live oak tree and dismounting said: "I guess this will do Phil, you make a fire while I go and get something for supper." The horses were staked out, Phil gathered wood and Wallace, taking a gun, went to some thick timber several hundred yards off. At dusk the crack of the rifle was heard and Wallace soon came back with a large turkey gobbler. This he split open putting each half on a large forked stick, giving Hodges one to cook and he took the other. When it was cooked the old pioneer ate nearly all of his half without bread or salt. He then lay down on his saddle blanket and slept soundly until daybreak, then was up ready to finish his turkey and be off again. Hodges followed suit in all these things.

As a farmer on the Medina, Wallace was not successful. He made several failures. In one crop he got Jeff Bond to go in with him and they planted forty acres of corn but it was another dry year and the corn failed except nine nubbins. One day while Jeff was away, Wallace determined to have the benefit of those nine small roasting ears before they got too hard to eat, and went out and gathered them. He cut the corn all nicely off the cob, then putting some bear grease in the frying pan, cooked them. When he went to sit down to his repast the thought struck him that Jeff owned a half interest in that crop and should have his part. So he drew a line through the fried corn and only ate his side, and put the balance away for his partner. The absent man, however, did not get his share. Sam Lytle came along hungry and finished it despite the protest of Bigfoot who told him how the case stood. The Lytles had moved in there and settled on the Medina below. Charley Lytle died and was buried there, and his little dog would not leave his grave.

Wallace would go from his cabin every day and carry the dog something to eat. The dog would sit by the grave and look at it as if he expected his master to come out.

After the country began to settle, many people got lost and Wallace would hunt for them and was always successful. A little girl was lost once and Bigfoot hunted several days but there was so much prickly pear and chaparral the child was hard to find. One evening, however, he saw a Mexican Quihi (eagle) light on the ground on the side of a rocky hill. Going to the spot, he found the child but she was dead.

On another occasion Sam Lytle, then a boy, got lost and Wallace found him.

A man named Jones had a fight with the Indians at his house and told Wallace that he shot two of them badly and that his dogs tore up another. Wallace took the trail of the Indians, although the trail was old, and found two dead Indians covered with leaves and sticks. Wallace knew Indian ways so well. It was not difficult for him to find their camp or their dead if they lost any in battle.

During his stay on the Medina, Wallace made one fine crop of corn and sold it for a good price. He also served under Jack Hays again as a ranger. Their camp was near the cabin of Wallace, so he was at home and in the service too.

The Lipan Indians were friendly then and lived on the Francisco west of the Medina. Their chief was named Juan Castro after his father of the same name who served in the Spanish army in Mexico and got his name there. The old chief died near Austin.

The chief who lived on Francisco had a daughter named "Chepeta" who often came with others to the cabin of Wallace and was very fond of him. Wallace treated her well and taught her to speak English. She called him "Mucho Grande Capetan Wallaky."

CHAPTER XX

MEXICAN WAR OF 1846 - FIGHT WITH THE LIPAN INDIANS.

While Bigfoot Wallace was a ranger, a treaty was made with the Comanche Indians at Fort Belknap. A portion of the men under Hays was sent there to be on hand in case of a rupture. Ad Gillespie, one of the rangers, was along who had been in the fight at the Pinta trail crossing of the Guadalupe and on that occasion had shot an Indian in a hand to hand struggle, and in turn had been lanced by the Comanche. Each thought the other could not survive the wound that had been given when the drawn battle was over, and both quit the field.

While the treaty was in progress, Gillespie laid down and went to sleep. Wallace soon after noticed an Indian standing near and intently gazing on the face of the sleeping ranger. Not knowing what his intentions were, Bigfoot walked up and asked the Comanche why was looking at the sleeping man. The Indian told of the fight at the Pinta trail crossing and showing the scar where he was wounded, said he was the man who did it. He also said he wounded the white man with a lance and could put his finger on the spot. Wallace told him to do so. He complied and said "there" as he indicated a place with his finger. Gillespie now waked up and Wallace said "Take a look at your old partner Ad." Explanations now followed and Gillespie laughing said "He must be the chap," and showed the old lance wound. The Comanche took off his blanket and showed the bullet wound on his brawny chest.

These treaties which were made with the hostile Indians at that and other times were not of long duration. The Indians would steal horses and that would bring on a collision again between them and the whites and all would soon be on the warpath again. The treaties really did no good and only caused the settlers to be off their guard when the Indians came on a raid.

When the Mexican war of 1846 broke out, Jack Hays raised a regiment of rangers for service in Mexico. Many of his old comrades raised companies for the regiment. Among those were Kit Ackland, Mike Chevalier, Ad Gillespie, Ben McCulloch and others. Samuel H. Walker, who figured in the Mier Expedition, was Lieutenant Colonel. Wallace joined the company of Gillespie and went out as 2d Lieutenant.

This regiment of Texas troops did good service in Mexico. Many of them had old scores to settle with the Mexicans. Only three years before, some in the regiment had drawn for their lives and worked on the streets in chains, footsore and nearly starved.

Wallace was in all the fighting around Monterrey and in the desperate assault on the Bishop's Palace where his captain was killed. Early on that foggy morning, when the demonstrations were to be made on the palace, Captain Gillespie and Lieutenant Wallace went close to the walls of the fort to investigate. While they were there the fog lifted. Wallace fired and killed a Mexican sergeant who was standing near. About this time Gillespie slipped on a rock, fell against the wall of the fort and was shot by a sentinel. The ball struck the pistol lock of the Captain and splitting, one half of it went through his body. Wallace conveyed him to the rear, out of the battle which was now coming on.

The Mexicans made a bold fight but were finally routed and their cannon all dismounted. They have some superstition about their defeat at the Bishop's Palace and the old rusty cannon are still lying where the Americans dismounted them. Soldiers are on duty there day and night and have been ever since the battle.

Captain Gillespie lived twenty-two hours after being wounded, and suffered a great deal, being shot through the bowels. He drank water all the time, but morphine was administered and he died easy.

At the winding up of the battle while the bugles were sounding a parley and the Mexicans were surrendering, Wallace was seen to aim his gun at a Mexican who had a flag. Officers interfered and one of them said "Lieutenant, don't you know a parley when you hear it blowed?" Wallace said "No! Not when I am in front of that man." The Mexican in question was the man who held the bean pot when the Texans were drawing for their lives at Salado, and called up other Mexicans to look at the big hand of Wallace, and in various ways tantalized the wretched men. Wallace now accosted him in thundering tones and asked him if he had any bean lottery here now. "Look at that hand. Do you know it? Ever see it before?" The Mexican said "No." "Yes, you did," said Bigfoot, "and called up others to look at it." He then cursed the Mexican for all the lowdown cowards he could think of, who only hung his head and as Wallace expressed it, "Looked like a coyote."

Part of the rangers were sent back to Texas for frontier protection after Taylor's battles were over and of this lot was Wallace. When his term of enlistment was out, he went back to his old cabin on the Medina.

In 1848 Joseph Blair Wallace, brother of Bigfoot, arrived from the old home in Virginia and they had a fine time together hunting and scouting. Joseph served three months as a ranger, but his eyesight being defective, he soon afterward returned to Virginia, leaving a fine flintlock rifle with Bigfoot.

Although the Indians who lived on the Francisco had been friendly, the time came when they had trouble with the white settlers who had commenced to settle west of the Medina and which ended in an open rupture. A fight or two took place and Lipans moved into the mountain country towards the Northwest and made many raids on the whites. In one of these raids they got a mule and horse of Bigfoot Wallace, besides many horses and mules belonging to other settlers. This was in 1848.

The pioneers naturally looked to Wallace to lead them against the Indians and were surprised at his delay, for a month passed away before he took any steps to follow and chastise them. He said the Indians soon after a raid would be on the watch out and hard to surprise. He wanted to wait until they fancied they were not to be followed and were careless, and then "pounce" on them.

When the Lipans arrived at their camp which was at what is now called "Frio Water Hole" on the divide at the head draws of the river, "Chepeta," the chief's daughter, recognized the horse and mule of Wallace and was greatly agitated, and warned her people to look out, that Bigfoot would be after them sure.

When Wallace thought the time had arrived to go on an expedition against the Indians, the first thing he did in getting ready was to mount his horse and wend his way through the chaparral and prickly pear many miles towards the southwest until he pulled rein at the cabin door of his friend Edwin Dixon Westfall who lived the life of a hermit on the banks of the Leona River far in advance of civilization.

Westfall was equal to Wallace or any other partisan leader as guide trailer or fighter. He was tall, straight and strong of limb, and had no mortal fear of man or beast. He and Bigfoot had been on many dangerous trips together and each knew the courage and ability of the other.

Westfall saw Wallace as soon as the latter emerged from the brush and entered the clearing of several acres surrounding the cabin, and when he approached, cried out "Hello Foot git down. Glad to see you." "Same to you" was the reply. "What's the news." As they shook hands Westfall answered "Nothing stirring here, what's the matter down the country?" "Indians!" said Wallace.

The two friends sat up late that night and Wallace gave particulars of the Lipan raid and his plans for the expedition and the help that was expected from Westfall. The latter was more than willing to go, had heard of the raid, and was surprised that Wallace had not been after them before now, but said it was all right, that they would "catch them napping." No great amount of preparation was necessary. A few more bullets molded, powderhorn replenished, and all was ready for the start early next morning. The two pioneers wended their way back a distance of fifty miles to the cabin of Bigfoot and soon began to raise men for the Indian hunt.

Westfall's ranch was on the Leona thirty miles below the present town of Uvalde and completely isolated from the balance of the world.

Wallace and Westfall raised about thirty men and the start was made towards the northwest. All trails by this time had been obliterated and the Indians had to be searched for.

The route lay up the Medina to where Bandera is now, then through the famous pass of Bandera and over into the Guadalupe valley, up that stream past where Kerrville is now and out to the head of the Guadalupe River. Wallace knew that if he could get within a radius of twelve or fifteen miles of the hostile camp he could find it. Hunting parties would be out in various directions and if he crossed their trails the main body could be found.

At the head of the Guadalupe Indian sign was plentiful; some being quite fresh. Wallace secreted his men and horses, and he and Westfall went alone and on foot. An old trail, but large, was discovered going in the direction of the head draws of the Frio River in a southwest course. Numerous single trails were seen going in the same direction and late in the evening a lone Indian was discovered riding across the divide south. Wallace also with a spyglass detected a smoke in a valley and the forms of two Indians about it. They were squaws smoking bees out of a tree and getting the honey.

The two scouts went back to the men and remained there that night. Early the next morning they got out of the canyon and cut across the rocky divide in a post oak and black jack country towards the head of the Frio, going clear around the draws of the Medina, Seco and Sabinal, which all head close together against the divide which runs between these streams and the South Llano and its tributaries. Also on the south side of this divide head the two Frios, Nueces and many small creeks.

The divide is undulating, interspersed with timber and prairie, and all covered with rocks. Unmistakable signs of the near approach to an Indian encampment were seen at various places and about noon a smoke was again seen.

The men were now in the timber and the smoke was a little south of them at the head of the east prong of the main Frio. Wallace now enjoined the utmost caution on the part of the men and led them down an open draw with timbered ridges on both sides. Soon a noise of numerous horses moving was heard on the ridge to the south. Wallace quickly dismounted, handed his bridle rein to a man, told the balance to halt and lightly ran up the incline until he could look over. Here he discovered a large drove of horses moving through the timber followed by two Indian boys.

Bigfoot took in the situation at once. These horses belonged to the Indian encampment, had been carried out to graze and were now being driven to water. The camp was close. The smoke was coming out of a draw close by and the horses were going straight towards it, and even now some of them had begun to disappear into it. Wallace trotted back to his men, hastily informed them of the situation, said this was the time to charge, and mounting his horse, dashed up the ridge, Westfall at his side and the balance following. His idea was to charge in behind the loose horses and the clatter they made would drown the noise made by their own horses, and more effectually surprise the Indians.

It was as Wallace had anticipated. Never before were Indians more surprised. The two young Indians fled in another direction without giving the alarm.

The Indians' camp was in a draw of the Frio at a large waterhole fed by a spring and the Indians were all engaged in a feast of buffalo meat which the hunters had brought in. Their shields and bows were lying about on the ground or hanging in trees when the onset was made.

The settlers went into the camp on horseback at a full running charge making a great deal of noise, stampeding the Indians' horses which greatly added to the confusion.

Just as they entered the camp, the mare rode by Wallace struck her foot against a rock and fell, throwing him over her head. Bigfoot lit on his feet

half bent, but such was his momentum, he could not check up for several yards and came near butting an Indian in the stomach with his head, who had commenced to run away. Wallace had brought the gun which his brother had left with him on this trip, a strong, heavy flintlock, and before he got erect, aimed it at the Indian and attempted to fire, but instead of exploding the piece, the flint flew into atoms. In vain the Indians tried to rally and get into position to fight. They were overrun and crushed by Westfall and the balance of the men and soon scattered in wild flight.

Great confusion prevailed. Nearly 200 head of horses and mules were stampeding around them. Rifles were cracking, Indians yelling and whistling bullets cut the air on every side. Wallace was furious, time and again he tried to fire his rifle and almost placed the muzzle of the piece against the Indians who were running by him and ascending the hill in his rear toward the deep gorges of the Frio.

During this wild scene he heard a shrill voice screaming "El Capetan! El Capetan! Wallaky! Wallaky!" It was the voice of Chepeta, as she came bounding like a deer through the stampeding horses and fighting men to the side of Wallace for protection. He told her to take hold of the tail of his buckskin hunting shirt and swing on to him and she would be safe. She did so during the balance of the fight, turning and whirling as he did. During this time, however, Wallace says there was one man so green that it was a wonder that the cows had not eaten him ere this. Seeing the action of Chepeta, he ran up and aiming his gun at her, exclaimed, "Look! Wallace, Look! There is one got hold of your coat tail!" and would have shot her had not the girl with dextrous movement kept Wallace between herself and the deadly rifle. Bigfoot turned on the man and yelled "Damn you, can't you see this is a girl and not trying to hurt me!"

The fight was not of long duration. The Indians were soon scattered and out of sight, except ten who were killed. At the wind up of the battle, Wallace saw an Indian on foot some distance off, carrying a gun in his hand and a shield between his shoulders. There was one corner of Wallace's flint left and aiming high, took a last chance at him. To his surprise, the gun fired and the Indian fell. The ball struck the shield near the top and having a solid brace against the back, went through and broke the Indian's spine, killing him instantly. Wallace got his gun, a very good flintlock, and afterward had it changed to a percussion. Many shields, bows and moccasins were obtained. One shield was decorated with the caudle appendages of two rattlesnakes which had thirty-two rattles each upon them. The horses and mules, 190 in number, were collected but Wallace's mule and horse were not there. Chepeta said some of the Indians had them on a buffalo hunt. The Indian maid bewailed the slaughter of her people, but Wallace told her "not to take on," and stay there until some of them came back. She was left in camp with one old squaw.

CHAPTER XXI

CHOLERA IN SAN ANTONIO. CARRY THE MAIL TO EL PASO.

In 1849, while Captain Wallace was living on the Medina, the cholera broke out and raged fearfully in San Antonio.

Wallace had some friends living in town and went twice a week to see how they were getting along. Dr. Cupples, who lived in Castroville, and who had been a surgeon in the French army under Napoleon Bonaparte, went to the afflicted city to treat cholera patients. He told Wallace that if he would come in during the day and leave before night, there would be no danger. The cholera germ arose in the air when the sun rose and settled back at night. Wallace says that when he was on his way to town and ascended the hill on the Leon, nine miles from town, he could always see a dense cloud hanging over the place and when the sun would go down the cloud settled.

On one occasion he went in on Sunday and more people died on that day than ever before, and it was called "Black Sunday." On that day dogs, chickens and hogs died. People fled in terror towards the mountains and many died on the prairies before they could reach them.

Captain Wallace says that Dr. Cupples told him the mesquite tree, so plentiful in West Texas, was identical to the gum arabic tree of Egypt. There was no difference in them. Leaves and all were exactly alike.

In this same year Wallace went on an exploring expedition across the plains. They suffered at times for food and had to live on prairie dogs. They had no trouble with the Indians as the cholera had got among them and they had scattered off into small bands, with their war spirit considerably dampened.

In 1850, Wallace obtained a contract to carry the mail from San Antonio to El Paso, a distance of 600 miles and frontier all the way. Five hundred miles of the way was entirely unsettled and it took one month to make a trip.

During the time he carried the mail, which covered a period of several years, he had many exciting adventures with the Indians. He had mounted guards, six in number, who always rode close up to the rear of the stage so there would be no chance for the Indians to make a dash from cover and cut them off and capture the loose mules which were always carried along in case of accident.

On one occasion however, in the Devils River country, one of the guards named Ben Sanford dropped a short distance behind and was shot with an arrow by an Indian who was secreted near the road behind a Spanish dagger. He was so close Sanford heard the twang of his bowstring when the Indian turned the arrow loose. The wounded man ran his mule up to the side of the stage and told Wallace he had been shot by an Indian and expressed a belief that his wound was fatal. The stage was at once stopped, the guards ordered back to kill the Indian and Sanford taken from the mule and lifted inside the stage. Wallace pulled the arrow out and perceived that the man was badly hurt.

The hunt by the guards was unsuccessful for the Indian and the journey was resumed. Sanford suffered great pain and died in the stage the next day. Wallace kept on until he saw the man was dead and then stopped and buried him.

Captain Wallace says that while he was on this mail route a large outfit came to El Paso on their way to California. They were led by a man named Finch and had many ambulances and wagons. They broke up in El Paso and scattered, some going into Mexico. Some of them came back nearly starved and Wallace helped to feed them.

On one of these trips Wallace encountered very cold weather. The road was full of ice and cut the mules feet so badly that he took them off the stage and crossing the Rio Grande, carried the mail around through Mexico to its destination. This was the nearest route and the ice was not so bad in the road. On this trip he was twenty-four hours without anything to eat and when he arrived at a little town opposite El Paso, stopped at a restaurant and asked the proprietor how much he charged for breakfast. "Twenty-five cents" was the answer.

"All right," said Wallace. "Bring plenty of eggs."

The Mexican only had eight, but Bigfoot said he must do better than that. He looked at Wallace and then went and hustled all he could, making a total of twenty-seven. He was told to go to cooking now, that would be sufficient. The Mexican, however, hesitated and seemed perplexed about something. It would near about break him up in business to cook so many eggs for twenty-five cents. Wallace, apprehending the situation, relieved his fears by handing over a dollar and then told him to "pitch in quick." This had the desired effect and the steaming eggs and other eatables were soon before the hungry Texan.

Wallace says it was a "Pretty good batch," but he managed to get away with all of them. It was quite a curious proceeding, however, to the onlookers who gathered around and looked at the "Mucho Grande Americano" who could eat so many eggs.

Feeling greatly refreshed, Wallace continued the journey to El Paso and then went back on the

Texas side, got his stage, and returned to San Antonio.

CHAPTER XXII

INDIAN FIGHT ON DEVILS RIVER.

The hardest fight with Indians which Bigfoot Wallace and his guards had while running the mail line occurred just above the painted cave at the crossing on Devils River.

The bluffs are high here and a capital place for Indians to ambush travelers on the road.

The stage party had stopped for noon and were just preparing to renew their journey when twenty-seven Comanche Indians attacked them from the bluff. Wallace and his party of six, including himself, at once commenced a defense, but the Captain soon told them to hold their fire and save bullets as the Indians were so well protected among the rocks that it was a waste of lead to shoot at them. It was hard for the men to keep from shooting when being fired on both by bullets and arrows, but Bigfoot said, "keep cool, they will show themselves directly, when they find out we will not shoot." This state of affairs was kept up some time and the Indians thinking the white men were cowards, began to partially show themselves. "Now, boys!" exclaimed Wallace, "run and tumble down under the stage like you were nearly scared to death." This was done quickly and the Indians yelled, called them cowards and squaws. The chief told his men that they could go down there and scalp all of them, as they would not fight. The men lay quiet and the Indians continued to fire on them and to heap vile epithets. Many arrows were shot and three hit the stage and remained fastened there. While others went over, some fell short, sticking in the ground in a few feet of the wheels. One bullet hit a tire on the stage, split, and half of it wounded Adolph Fry in the breast, but not seriously. The names of some of the other men of the party were McAllister, Gideon Scallaron, Louis Oge, and also one Mexican, name not known. Soon after the wounding of Fry, the chief and four of his braves came out in full view to take a good look at the situation, and Wallace said: "Now boys, every man for his Indian, take good aim, fire!" The rifles almost cracked as one and every Indian in sight fell.

The Indian chief dropped near the edge of the cliff and his arm hung over. Wallace yelled, and exclaimed, "There now, you are done eating horse meat."

For some time nothing was seen or heard of the Indians. Presently a lasso was seen to come over the rocks and fall among the dead men. "They are going to leave, boys, they have got enough of us," said Wallace, "but they don't want us to get those fellows' scalps. They are afraid to come to them and are going to rope and pull them behind the rocks." It was a slow business and many failures were made but loop after loop came until all were caught and dragged away except the one which hung over the cliff. Many failures were made at him, but at last a big loop came which dropped below his hanging arm and he was quickly pulled out of sight.

The Indians failed to show themselves anymore and Wallace hitched up the mules and started, but not for El Paso. He knew the Indians would ambush him again somewhere and likely with a larger force so he put back for Fort Clark.

The three arrows which stuck in the stage remained there a long time and were quite a curiosity to newcomers who looked at them when the stage arrived in San Antonio.

It was the intention of Wallace to get an escort of soldiers at Fort Clark and take his mail on through, but failing in this, had to come on to Fort Inge on the Leona, four miles below the present town of Uvalde. Here he failed again. The commander at that post said he was afraid his men would desert if he carried them to El Paso. Bigfoot then wrote a letter to the Department of San Antonio, and telling the officer at Fort Inge that they could all go to the devil, hired an escort on his own hook and went back with the mail.

General Kirby Smith, commander of the Department of Texas at that time, arrived in San Antonio about the time Wallace's letter reached there, and being mad at the way things had been managed, ordered the troops at Fort Inge on a long scout, nearly to the Mexico line. On the return trip Wallace met them and they looked as if they had, as he expressed it, "Been through the rubbers."

They had no tobacco and had been living on poor turkeys for several days. Wallace never failed to deliver his mail but once on an outgoing trip to El Paso. On that occasion, however, he lost all of his mules and his whole outfit had to leave the stage and walk to El Paso, a distance of 80 miles.

The circumstances were these: he had gone into camp at "Dead Man's Hole" and the mules had been turned out to graze with a guard to watch them. Wallace was sitting down near a big rock mending some of his harness, and hearing a slight movement over him, looked up and around quick and saw an Indian on the rock in ten feet of him, just bringing his gun around to shoot. Big Foot threw up his pistol to shoot and the Indian dodged back out of sight. He now also perceived that the guards had strayed off and a band of Indians were driving off the mules. In vain he yelled for them to save the mules, but it was too late. They could only fire at them at long range as the hostiles ran away with the stock, yelling back at them.

The only chance was to walk back to El Paso and get more team and come back after the stage.

"Dead Man's Hole" derived its name from the circumstance of two United States soldiers being killed there by Indians. Wallace found their remains and torn uniforms there when he first began to run the line.

On one occasion on Devils River, Wallace found a track in the road that greatly puzzled him. He alighted from the stage and closely examined it. It looked something like a bear track but it was too long and wide. "It is not an Indian" says Wallace to the guards. "They have some shape and symmetry to their moccasins. It steps like a damn black slave, but what in the devil has he got on, and what is he doing out here in this wilderness if it is one?" Not far from there Wallace camped for the night and the strange individual came to them. He was a negro and a runaway at that and nearly starved.

The negro was crawling up to the camp and one of the mules snorted at him. Wallace ran around a rock to see what it was and came near to shooting him. The negro sprang to his feet and said, "Don't shoot! Don't shoot! Fo God master I's glad to see you." Wallace said, "Come here, what sort of a man are you anyhow? Want to steal my mule don't you?" He expressed his entire innocence of any such intention and was soon relating his checkered experience.

He said that he had run away from his master in Louisiana and was trying to get to Mexico. He had been captured by Indians but made his escape and was almost naked and barefoot. The strange foot gear which he had on was made out of a piece of mule hide which the Indians had killed. It was stitched together and run to a point twice the length of a man's foot and had corners to it.

Wallace took him to El Paso where he furnished him clothing and blankets and also wrote his master to come to San Antonio after him. Wallace brought him back and put him in jail until he was turned over to his master, who had to pay for the clothing and blankets and $200, which was allowed for all fugitive slaves taken up west of the Medina River.

CHAPTER XXIII

WESTFALL KILLS THE BIGFOOT INDIAN.

On one return trip, and when near Fort Inge, Wallace discovered something in the road that he was very familiar with, but which he had not seen for a long time.

This was the track of the famous Bigfoot Indian and he had six followers with him. Wallace knew that his presence meant that all the horses in the country that he could round up would be carried off.

When the stage arrived at Fort Inge, Westfall was there and was told about the Indians by Wallace, who advised him to be on the lookout, that the country would be cleaned up of horse stock sure. Wallace had some mules that he always left at Fort Inge until he returned from San Antonio, but on this occasion ordered them carried east of the Frio and kept there. Before leaving he told Westfall where his mules would be and in case the Indians got all the horses, and men could not be mounted to follow them, to go and get his mules and use them. He also told Westfall if he killed Bigfoot he wanted his moccasins.

As Wallace expected, the settlers were careless and the Indians got nearly all the horses in the country and got off with them. Westfall, however, followed out the instructions of Wallace and was soon on the trail of the redskins, on the mules. The trail led up the Nueces Canyon, then not settled, to the divide and then turned across towards the head of South Llano. Westfall and his men followed on and one evening camped in the cedar brakes, being satisfied of the near proximity of the Indians. The utmost caution and silence were preserved. Westfall only had three men and one boy with him, making five in all. The boy was named Preston Polly and one of the men was Gideon Scallaron. The names of the others cannot now be ascertained. Westfall spent a wakeful night for he was satisfied the Indians were near and a fight would come off in the morning.

Just at the break of day a smoke was seen ascending above the cedar tops in the thickest part of the brake, not far from the settlers' camp. Westfall, who had stepped away from the camp a short distance to listen for any sound that might be heard in the still early hour, hastily retraced his steps and telling his companions what he had seen, took the boy Preston and went to reconnoiter the vicinity of the smoke.

The Indians had no thought that white men were near, in fact they did not suppose they had left horses enough for anyone to follow them on. Such would have been the case but for the keen sagacity and forethought of Bigfoot Wallace in having his mules hidden and telling Westfall where they were in case he needed them.

Wallace always craved to kill the Bigfoot Indian, more especially after he had killed his friend and companion Fox. While the end of the wily chief was near, and he was to fall by the hand of Edward Westfall, it was at least by the instrumentality of Bigfoot Wallace.

When Westfall left his men he told them in case they heard his rifle to come at once. He then went down a steep bluff and carefully picked his way through tall coarse grass, high as his head, to a point opposite the Indian encampment which was on high ground in a dense cedar brake. There was also a pool of water there and Westfall noticed a trail leading from it up the hill towards the point where he had seen the smoke. He was just about to start up this trail when he saw an Indian's legs through the brush and soon discovered a large fellow coming down towards the water leading a horse.

Westfall was a man of strong nerve but his heart beat quick when he saw the noted Bigfoot Indian before him. Making a silent gesture for the boy behind him to be still, he aimed his rifle through the tall grass and took a careful aim at the big savage. About this time the horse which Bigfoot was leading suddenly stopped and snorted as he detected the presence of Westfall. The Indian turned his head quick to look at the horse, presenting a side view of his body to the marksman in the ravine who instantly fired, and this scourge of the frontier fell hard on the ground. The three men of the camp when they heard the keen whip-like crack of Westfall's rifle break the stillness of the early morning, came yelling and almost tumbling down the embankment, giving assurance to their leader that help was near if he needed it.

The boy Preston stood by Westfall with a gun in his hand during this exciting scene with the utmost coolness for one of his years. The old pioneer hastily but steadily reloaded his gun and when his men joined him, led the way and rapidly advanced into the cedar brake, past the body of the dead chief to attack the Indian camp. The shot, however, and the answering yell of Westfall's men had struck terror to the band and they had fled, leaving their chief to his fate.

Everything about the camp indicated they were about to leave. A bear had been killed, barbecued and packed ready for traveling. Blankets, buffalo skins and one bow and quiver of arrows were left in camp. The stolen horses were also left except those the Indians went away on. It is surmised that

Bigfoot was carrying his horse down to water before making the start.

Westfall's men had eaten nothing since starting the trail so they did ample justice to the well cooked bear meat.

When the body of the fallen chief was approached it was found that the bullet had struck him in the left arm without breaking the bone, passed through the heart and body and came out through the right arm. In his right hand, tightly clutched, was a bow and some arrows, while the left hand held the rope attached to the horse. Such was the strong grip on both it was with difficulty that they could be released. The horse reared and plunged when the Indian fell but such was his weight that the frightened animal could not move him. The horse belonged to Adolph Fry and had been stolen at Fort Inge.

Westfall had promised Bigfoot Wallace the moccasins of the Bigfoot Indian and secured them for that purpose. When everything was collected up that they wished to carry. they went back to where they left the little mules of Wallace and were soon on their way back to Fort Inge, where they returned the stolen stock to the settlers.

Wallace had gone to El Paso with the stage so Westfall left the moccasins at the fort to be delivered to him on the return trip. They were a great curiosity and many people came to look at them on account of their size being nearly fifteen inches in length and beautifully decorated with beads. A man named John Wilkinson who had been around Fort Inge for some time, got possession of them by saying he was going down to San Antonio and would deliver them to Wallace there. Bigfoot was told about the Indian being killed on his arrival at the fort and that he could get the moccasins as soon as he arrived at San Antonio. He was however, disappointed, for Wilkinson had left and gone to the Brazos carrying them with him. Wallace wrote several letters in regard to them but of no avail. The man carried them on to the states with him.

As there were a great many rattlesnakes in West Texas, the writer asked Captain Wallace in regard to the largest one he had seen. He said that while running the mail line one time in the Devils River country he saw a trail of a snake cross the road and told some of the guards to follow it up and kill it as he wanted to look at him. The old resident was soon found coiled up under a large cactus. He was killed and dragged back to the road. He was not so long but very large, about the size of an ordinary man's thigh. Wallace told one of the men to cut him open as he believed there was something in him. This was done and a full grown jack rabbit exhumed, which the snake apparently had just swallowed.

CHAPTER XXIV

A NIGHT ATTACK ON THE STAGE - A TERRIBLE GUN FIRED BY THE INDIANS.

On the next trip Wallace made after the big Indian was killed, he and his guards had a fight with the Indians. Early in the morning when the start was made for the Pecos country, Wallace told his men to brace themselves for a ninety mile drive that day. Many signs of Indians had been seen the evening before. Signal smokes far away in different directions, uneasiness of the mules at night, all combined, convinced the experienced frontiersman that on the following night an attempt would be made to capture the stage. His object in making this long drive before camping another night was to scatter the Indians who would follow them through the day.

He knew that all of their horses could not hold out on such a trip, and would only have part of the band to fight if any. All day the stage rattled along at a lively rate, the guards following, at times in a gallop.

A short halt was made at noon, mules fed and away again. At sundown it was ninety miles back to their last camp. During the day Wallace saw signs of pursuit in the distance, but knew nothing would be attempted until night.

In selecting a camp at night, he never stopped in high grass or very near thickets. The Indians would have no cover to advance close upon him unseen. The place selected for the night halt was in an open glade with short grass, but sufficient for the stock.

On one side and reaching partly around the camp was a thick chaparral sixty or seventy yards away. When night closed down, Wallace had all the mules placed or staked on the side of the stage farthest from the brush. Putting George Hubbard on guard, Wallace told the other men to lay down around and under the coach, having their guns and pistols ready. Wallace himself did not lay down, but with ever vigilant eye, scanned the dark circle of the brush so as to detect the least movement there.

Hours passed on and all was still as midnight on a desert plain except the cropping of grass by the hungry and tired mules. At length a raven arose from the chaparral with a startled "caw!" and with broad flapping wings, flew towards the mules and alighted on the head of the guard who was standing in the rear of the stage, motionless as a post. With a quick motion George ducked his head and uttered an exclamation which sounded in the dark like "Ellen Damnation." Some might have thought he was calling the name of his sweetheart as he stood the lonely vigils of the night, and his mind had wandered back to the loved ones at home, if he had not said it so quick and energetically.

Now George was of a slightly superstitious nature and the cold chills chased each other up and down his spine when he discovered that it was a raven which had lit on his head. He at once went to Wallace, informing him of the circumstances, and asked him its significance. "It means," says Wallace, "that the damned Comanches have overtaken us and are now in that chaparral brush over there. They have scared that raven off his roost, which in its flight across the open ground mistook the top of your head for a stump and lit on it; that's all."

Wallace had one mule that would never eat when Indians were around and this one now raised her head, blowed and looked straight towards the brush and refused to put her head to the ground anymore, but would walk to the end of the rope, then turn quick, snort, and look towards the brush again.

"They are here boys, handle your guns," said Wallace, as he pulled two long barreled brass dueling pistols and crouched close to a coach wheel, one in each hand and pointed towards the danger point.

The men were all on the alert and ready but still the Indians did not show up. Hours passed away again.

The guards began to relax and hunt easy braces for their backs and heads against the stage wheels, tongue, etc. Peter Weble stretched out full length on his back, his head resting between two spokes of the vehicle. Wallace remained immovable with the pistols still in hand and with constant moving eye surveying the dark rim of the brush from one point to another. The mules were all uneasy and stamping.

Presently three dark forms became detached from the brush and started across the opening. Others were seen in quick succession emerging from the chaparral at different points and gliding silently towards the stage.

Bigfoot gave one short command to "nip them quick," and levelled his pistol at the three foremost Indians. The whole band, who seeing now that they were discovered, began to yell and come at a charge with uplifted shields and sending a flight of arrows and bullets ahead of them.

Wallace had an eight shooting rifle which he caught up after throwing his pistols down, and began to pump lead into them with that.

The men took shelter behind the stage, firing under and around it and the Indians could not get to the mules without passing them. Their idea by this onset was to run them away from the stage out into the prairie and then secure the stock.

One Indian fired a large swell muzzled musket, called a blunderbuss, that would carry nearly a handful of powder and the same of buckshot. Wallace says it looked like a bushel of fire came out of it and the shot struck the stage like a sluice of hail.

About that time a terrible commotion was heard under the stage and the old vehicle rocked and rattled like it was in a hurricane. Peter Weble, who had laid his head between the spokes, had gone to sleep. He started to spring up when the fight commenced but had not remembered the position he occupied before going into the land of dreams. His head was fast between the spokes and he was making frantic efforts to disengage himself.

Bigfoot said that at one time he thought Weble was going to run clear off with the stage. Peter was brave, however, and as soon as he could get out of his predicament, joined in the fight and helped to repel the Indians, but his neck was sore for two or three weeks afterward. The battle was over in less time than it takes to write it. The Indians made one charge, and meeting such a fire, scattered and went back to the brush as quick as they came.

How many were killed is not known. The night was not very light and only the outlines of their forms could be seen. None of Wallace's men were hit, but the stage caught it heavy, both with bullets and arrows.

Wallace did not propose to give the Indians another chance at him that night, but at once harnessed up when the Indians were gone. Securing his pistols which had fallen by a coach wheel, he hit the road again, followed by the guards. When daylight came they were many miles from there.

During one of his trips the Apaches and the Mexicans had a good deal of trouble above El Paso. The chief of the Apaches was named "Blue Beads," whose camp was near town. One night when the old chief started back from town drunk, he was followed and killed by the Mexicans. Then the slaughter of the Mexicans commenced by the Apaches in revenge. They would have killed all of them but for the United States soldiers who put a stop to it.

The Apaches at that time were friendly with the whites. Wallace had started back on a return trip and had a Mexican aboard who lived in San Antonio. The stage was met by a large body of Apaches who surrounded and stopped it, and tried to kill the Mexican who was on the seat with Wallace. They made repeated thrusts at him with their lances which were warded off by Wallace with his gun. He told them that if they did not leave, he would order the guards to fire on them, as they were delaying the United States mail. The chief understood English, and soon galloped off with his men.

CHAPTER XXV

CAPTAIN OF RANGERS - FIGHT A BATTLE WITH THE INDIANS AT BLACK HILLS.

While Captain Wallace had many more incidents connected with his stage driving on the long frontier line from San Antonio to El Paso which could be of interest to the reader, the main facts have been given in the preceding chapters.

He tells of one instance of killing a black-tailed deer at the "Wild Rose Pass." It was an extra large buck with powerful horns, standing on the cliff and gazing down at the moving stage below. He was a fine mark to shoot at, but a long distance off, and a doubt was expressed of anyone being able to bring him down. Wallace said he could do it and taking careful aim, making allowance for the distance, fired. The big buck reared at the shot and then plunged headlong into the abyss below. His body made revolutions in the air as he descended, and, as Wallace expressed it, was mashed into "sausage meat" on the rocks at the bottom.

After Captain Wallace quit the mail service, he went back to his old cabin on the Medina, but did not remain long. People were moving in fast and settling around him, so one morning he packed up such things as he had and wanted to carry, got his rifle, and whistling up his dog, set out towards the southwest carrying all of his earthly possessions on a pack mule.

Captain Wallace always had plenty of money to purchase such things as he needed, but was not encumbered with much personal effects. In a wild and lonely spot on the Chicon Creek east of the Hondo River, and now distant about five miles from the present thriving little city of Devine, Bigfoot unloaded his pack and there built a cabin.

People were settling along the Hondo, Sabinal, Seco and other places and the Indians were constantly raiding upon them. The people soon found out where the cabin of Wallace was and looked to him as a leader in pursuit of Indians.

During one raid a messenger came from above and notified him that the Indians were going down the Hondo valley. Bigfoot got six men together, or five men, rather, and a boy, for Lon Moore was in the party and was only twelve years of age. The trail was closely and rapidly followed. The Indians were overtaken near San Miguel Creek. A fight ensued in which two Indians were killed and the balance scattered and turned up the country. Wallace had one man slightly wounded with an arrow.

One of the closest shaves Bigfoot Wallace ever had in his life was while in pursuit of a band of Indians. On this occasion he had gathered a few settlers and was following a trail through a brushy country. The Indians finding that they were being pursued, laid an ambush. Wallace was in the lead trailing when suddenly an Indian rose up in front of him not more than a few steps distant, with his gun aimed squarely at the Captain's breast.

It took quick thought and action to avoid the discharge but Wallace was equal to the occasion. He had his gun in hand ready to shoot at a moment's warning. The minute the Indian threw up his gun, Wallace threw himself backward from his horse. The bullet went over his head, and he at the same time shot the Indian from the ground where he lay.

J. M. Smith, who now lives near the Miguel post office, and who was one of the party, said it was the quickest work he ever saw done. The fall of Wallace from his horse, the fire of the Indian and shot from Bigfoot almost occurring simultaneously. Several Indians showed themselves, one of whom was shot by Smith, but not killed. The Indian Wallace shot, fell in his tracks, breathed and struggled a minute, and was then dead.

While P. H. Bell was governor of Texas, he commissioned Wallace to raise a company of rangers for the protection of Southwest Texas from incursions of hostile Indians. Seventy-six men were raised, among whom was Edward Westfall who afterwards served as lieutenant in the company. They were almost constantly in the saddle riding on many long scouts, and chasing, and sometimes having a skirmish. The Indians avoided a conflict as much as possible, dreading to meet Wallace and Westfall in battle. So well did they know them that a picture of Westfall was found on a rock in the mountains, drawn by the Indians, and which bore such a resemblance to the slayer of the Bigfoot Indian that it was recognized by the men who found it. Westfall was one inch taller than Wallace, but of slighter build. He had light hair and blue eyes.

The hardest fight that Wallace and his men had while he was captain in the ranging service occurred at a place called "Black Hills," sixteen miles from the present town of Cotulla in La Salle County. Wallace had been on a long scout down the country with nineteen men and was coming back. It was a very dry year in the month of August in the early 50's and the men were suffering intently with thirst as the water holes had dried up where they expected to find water. Wallace and Westfall knew where all the watering places were and went from one to the other, only to find hard mud or glistening white rocks. To add more to their discomfort, one of the rangers named Jackson was very sick. He was unable to ride his horse and had to be carried on a stretcher which necessarily made their progress very slow.

All this time the sky was like brass over their heads. The August sun poured its scorching rays upon them day by day as they toiled along. Finally Captain Wallace said he knew where there were water holes on the "Todas Santos" (All Saints) Creek in the Black Hills that certainly had water in them as they were never known to be dry. Across to the Black Hills the rangers turned and finally came in view of the coveted spot. They were eager to advance but Wallace held them back and ordered a halt. There were horses there and he did not like the look of things.

This surmising did not last long. The water was in possession of a large band of Comanche Indians. As soon as they discovered the approach of the rangers, they swarmed out towards them, about 80 in number, yelling loudly. Captain Wallace supposed he would be charged at once, as the Indians were so numerous. He gave orders sharply and quickly. "Dismount men, secure your horses, place Jackson under this mesquite tree here out of the way, and stay by your horses. Quick! Now quick! Here they come!" It seemed at first that the Indians were going to come at once and engage the rangers at close quarters, but when they saw the levelled rifles and the two conspicuous leaders, they weakened, and soon came to a standstill, despite the fact that their chief who seemed to be brave, waved his hand and urged them on, coming nearly within gunshot himself before turning back. Captain Wallace said "Boys they won't fight, they are cowards." The chief went among them, talked and gesticulated a great deal and then charged at full speed.

A few followed at a short distance, then wheeling, went back to the main body. Captain

Wallace advanced forward with a few men and took a position and again waited. "Now boys" said he, "when that chief comes again we must kill him, and the battle will be over. Three of you stand ready, and if he comes close enough, kill his horse, and I will kill him before he can get away. One of you shoot at his leg and break it if you can, and then we will be certain of him." Wallace had a large heavy rifle which once belonged to Colonel James Bowie who was killed in the Alamo. One pound of lead only made sixteen bullets for it.

Up to this time no shots had been fired. The chief would drop behind his horse when charging and ride back in that way when his men failed to come. The chief again harangued his warriors and came to the charge, not even looking back to see if they were coming. This time the brave old chief came within gun shot, and seeing some of the rangers about to fire, dexterously threw himself on the opposite of his horse.

Three rifles cracked about the same time and the horse fell dead in his tracks. The chief quickly regained his feet, not being hit himself, and looked for his braves to see if they were coming to his assistance. About this time Captain Wallace shot the chief through both hips and he fell. As he struck the ground he uttered two loud peculiar whoops which was answered by his cowardly men, and this time they came to him. The rangers met them with a charge and a fight took place. Captain Wallace noticed the rangers had left their horses and Jackson too far in the rear. He told them to get back as the Indians would make a dash and get them.

While this was being done, the Indians thought the rangers were giving way, and charged. For a time things were mixed. The rangers got to their horses and a good many of them mounted and

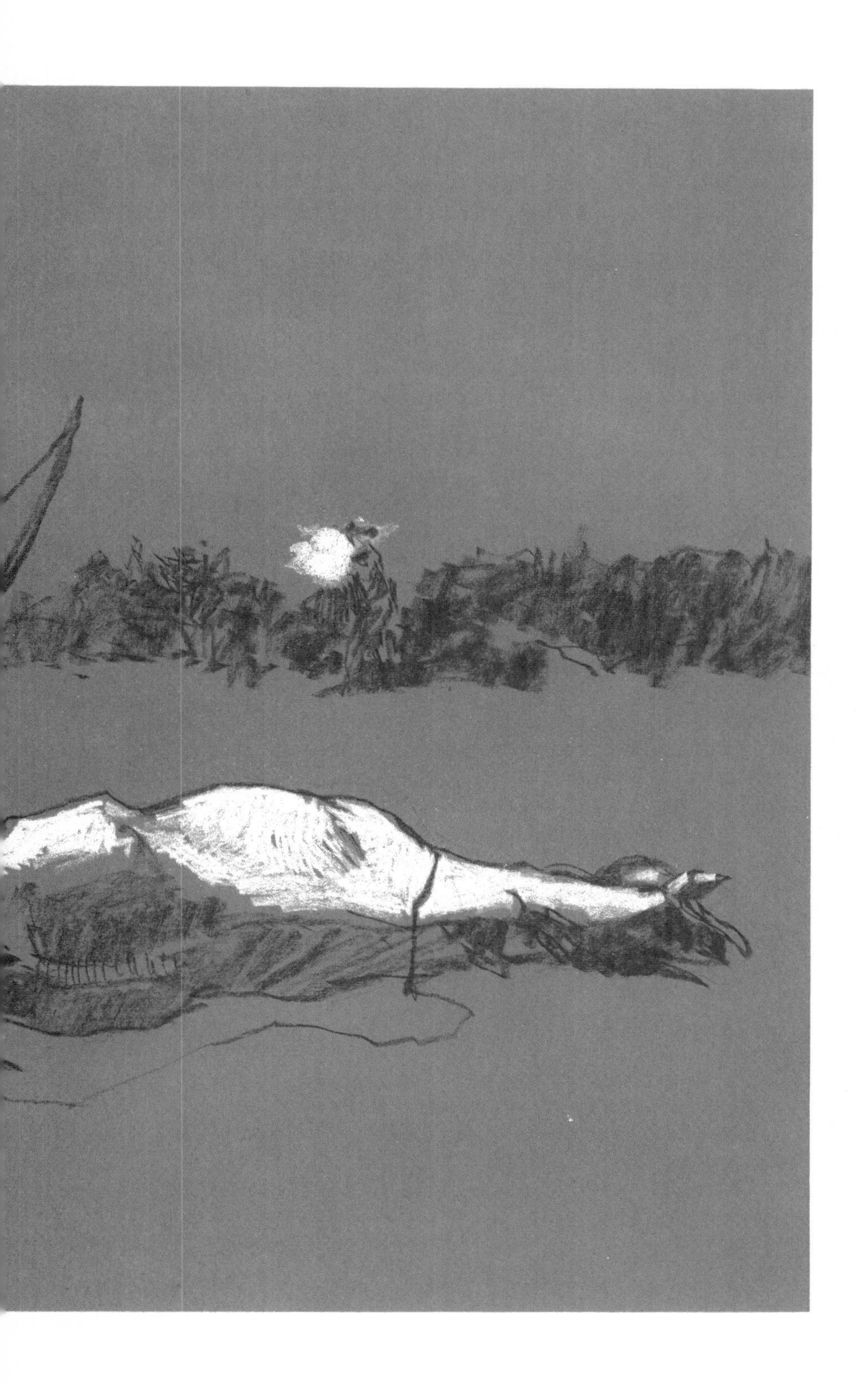

charged among the Indians, using their pistols.While this was going on, an Indian ran close to Jackson and looked at him, thinking he was dead.

The sick ranger was somewhat nerved up on account of the battle and turning his gun towards the Indian, fired at him.

The chief died on the ground where he fell and the Indians went back to the water hole, some of them on foot as their horses had been killed. Captain Wallace told his men they must follow them to the water and fight them again as some of the men were nearly ready to sink with thirst.

The Indians had for some purpose built a brush fence around the water, and when the rangers came to it at a charge, had to again dismount and tie their horses. Wallace and Westfall were the first at the brush. Wallace shot an Indian who was trying to run away and hastily reloaded his gun while others were crossing the brush, firing at different points.

When Captain Wallace rammed his ball down and capped his gun, an Indian sprang up a little to one side. Wallace quickly turned his gun to shoot him, holding the ramrod in his hand, not having time to replace it. It happened that Westfall at that time ran in close to the side of Wallace and the end of the gun stick struck him in the eye and nearly put it out. The pain was so great and he was so badly blinded for a time, Westfall held his head down with his hand clapped over the injured optic.

Another ranger came by at this time and asked Westfall if he was wounded. "No," he said, "Captain Wallace has put out one of my eyes with his gun stick at a time when I needed them the most."

One ranger in the fight named William Johnson, who always killed an Indian in a close place, shot one in the back as he was running up the bank of the creek. When the Indian fell, several pieces of tobacco fell out of his rigging. Captain Wallace passed by this place at a trot, but seeing the tobacco, stopped and picking it up, crammed some of it in his mouth. The rangers had been out of tobacco several days as well as water and the captain was an inveterate chewer.

There was another water hole above the camp and all the Indians went to that. The famished men, after routing the Indians, made a rush for the water but what was their horror to find they could not drink it unless it was a life or death case. The Indians had been there a week or more, making lariats, and soaked the rawhide in the pool which was already low, until the water was one seething mass of putrefaction — hair, maggots, etc.

Wallace saw it was impossible for men to drink that water and ordered a charge after the Indians at the upper water hole. Captain Wallace and Westfall led the charge. When they got there, they found the Indians with their force together and waiting to give them battle. Wallace waited awhile for the other men to come, but as only ten made their appearance, it was not safe to make a charge. A return was made back to the water hole. Some of the men were still there. Two of them had been wounded and others were nearly dead with thirst and exhaustion. The sick men had high fever and constantly called for water. The captain informed them of the situation and all who could, went back to fight the Indians.

Wallace said he was going to have a drink of water if he had to fight Indians all day for it. When the rangers got back to the water, a battle commenced at once, but a close charge led by Wallace and Westfall drove the Comanches away and were masters of the situation. When the men had quenched their thirst, canteens were filled, and they hastened back to their wounded and sick companions, and those who had remained with them.

While the men were drinking water from the canteens, one of the rangers told Captain Wallace that Luce Henyard, one of the rangers, was badly wounded and wanted to see him. The captain at once went to him and asked if he was badly hurt. He said, "Yes, I'm killed, Captain." He lay beside a tree, two rangers sitting down by him. His pale face was turned in a wishful look to that of his stalwart captain, who bent over him and began to examine his wound.

The ball had struck above the left hip and ranging a little down, had lodged in the right loin. The captain took a sharp knife and saying, "Cheer up my boy, I can fix you all right," proceeded to cut out the ball. Making two poultices of prickly pear, he put one over each wound.

The other ranger, Adolph Fry, had been hit by an arrow but was not so badly hurt. He was also treated to a pear poultice. Twenty-two Indians were killed in the fight.

Next morning, after the fight, Captain Wallace collected all the blankets, shields, bows, arrows, mules and horses, and set out for Fort Inge, where his sick and wounded men could get medical attention. The camp of the rangers at that time was at Westfall's ranch, twenty-seven miles below the fort. In a few days news came to Captain Wallace that his men, especially Henyard who had been wounded in the fight, were not doing well.

Wallace went up to the fort and found that the surgeon at the post had ignored his poultice of pears. He took his men away, carried them to the ranger camp and said he would cure them himself. He continued to poultice with prickly pears, which he says kept out all the fever and was the best for a wound of anything ever tried. His men at once began to improve and rapidly recovered.

CHAPTER XXVI

WESTFALL WOUNDED BY INDIANS.

When Captain Wallace quit the ranger service, he went back to his ranch on the Chicon and engaged in raising cattle and horses. His time, however, was divided in hunting, scouting after hostile bands of Indians, and trailing runaway negroes with his dogs. Slaves belonging to planters along the Brazos and Colorado rivers were continually escaping and trying to make their way into Mexico.

Wallace being in the woods so much of his time with his dogs, a negro could seldom pass near his cabin without being detected. He lived on the main route from San Antonio to the Rio Grande country and was as much on the lookout for negroes as Indians. He made considerable money apprehending negroes and getting the reward offered for them.

So famous had Bigfoot Wallace become as a slave catcher, that their owners would come to him for two hundred miles east and employ him to take his dogs and hunt them.

On one occasion two planters named Beck and Caldwell, who had lost negroes on the Colorado not far below Austin, came on southwest in search of them. When they arrived in San Antonio and made their business known, they were advised to proceed on out to where Wallace lived on the Chicon about fifty miles from San Antonio. This they did and after a good deal of trouble in finding the way, finally rode up to the door of the lonely little cabin in the wilderness and made their business known.

Wallace agreed to go with them, but expressed some doubt as to finding them, for said he: "I think you are ahead of them, or else they have went around my range." This, some of them did, when so many of them were caught by Wallace and carried back. They would tell the other negroes of the tall man who lived in the woods beyond San Antonio, and had dogs that could do everything but talk. They began to avoid this route and go through the mountains further north when running away.

Wallace took his dogs and going out with the wealthy guests, made a wide circle but no trace could be found. Not wishing, however, to give up yet, he told Beck and Caldwell of his friend Westfall, who lived a hermit's life still further southwest on the Leona River. They could go see him as he was out a great deal, and might give some information.

Westfall also had a lot of good dogs, one of which (and his favorite) was named George Washington.

At this time, however, Westfall was not without human companionship. A Frenchman named Louie had wandered away from the "pleasant land of France," and took up his abode in the wilderness with the Leona hermit.

On the way to the ranch Wallace killed a big fat deer and carried it along. No stop was made to eat anything since they left the place where they camped the night before, as they intended to rest and eat with Westfall. When in the neighborhood of the cabin, Wallace scanned the ground closely and remarked that he "did not like the looks of things." When asked why, he said Westfall generally walked about in the vicinity of his place every day moving his horses to grass or looking for Indian sign, and that he could see no fresh tracks. At last they emerged from the chaparral and came out into the clearing in the center of which was the cabin and corn cribs.

The first thing that attracted their attention when arriving at the yard fence was a dead man and a dead dog lying in the yard in front of the door. Wallace at once exclaimed: "Hello, the Indians have killed Westfall!" and springing from his horse, approached the body.

The dead man had tolerable long and very black hair. His face was swollen and as dark as that of an Indian. Wallace then said: "No, this is not Westfall; it is an Indian he has killed." On closer inspection, however, it was found to be the remains of the unfortunate Frenchman Louie and the dead dog was George Washington.

It was evident there had been a terrible fight here. Everything was torn up and the inside of the cabin was covered with blood, but Westfall was nowhere to be seen. Wallace went down to the river and gave some loud whoops, but no answer came. Everything was still as midnight on a desert plain.

The two planters stood around in silence, and with scared looks, surveyed the bloody scene. They were not used to these frontier tragedies and were now for their first time gazing on the bloody work of the savages. Wallace threw the deer from the horse, and telling them to start a fire and cook some of it, said he would take a round and see if he could find the trail of Westfall. About a mile from the house he found Westfall's track where it came into a trail and then led off towards Fort Inge, distant about thirty miles.

Wallace followed the trail far enough to learn that his friend was badly wounded, that he had a small dog with him, had on a pistol and water gourd, walked with a stick and had no gun. Some would like to know how Wallace knew these things without seeing Westfall. To him, with his knowledge of woodcraft, it was plain.

Westfall was badly wounded he knew from the short steps he took. The tracks of a small dog were following and the imprint of the stick was seen in the ground beside the tracks. He frequently laid down which was another sign of a severe wound and he also left the imprint of his pistol and water gourd in the soft soil of the trail where these halts were made. He was without a gun Wallace also knew as he could see no imprint of it where he laid down, as he would have placed it on the ground beside him when lying down.

Wallace returned to the cabin and telling the two men all these things, said he would follow after Westfall and help him. They had, however, cooked nothing, saying they were not hungry. Wallace said: "I'm a man who cannot go without eating when he can get it." He at once made a fire, broiled a good slice of venison on the coals, hastily ate it and prepared to start on his journey.

His two companions sat in gloomy silence, their eyes constantly wandering to the still form of the dead man in the yard.

Wallace was puzzled about Westfall's rifle. He could not find it anywhere. A shot gun was in the house, but this was all in the way of firearms. That the Indians did not enter the house after the fight, he knew. If they had they would have carried off the shot gun, and also killed Westfall, for the bed was bloody where he lay after being wounded.

Wallace told Beck and Caldwell that the slave hunt was off, and that they could go with him, or wend their way back to San Antonio. They chose the former and all three set out on the trail of Westfall. Many halts had been made by the stricken man, and he would build a small fire in the road occasionally. It was afterwards learned that he did this to make a little strong coffee in a can, which was all the nourishment he had during his painful journey of three days and nights to the fort. Wallace trailed Westfall to the very gate of the enclosure around the barracks and found that he had just arrived and was in the hands of the post surgeon.

Westfall was struck with a ball quartering on the left side just above the collar bone, grazing the juggler vein going through the right lung, and coming out below the right shoulder blade. Wallace says the juggler vein was exposed, disclosed by the ball, and badly swollen, so much so that it seemed a touch would burst it. He says he was shot from ambush while coming from a steel hand mill near the house where he had been grinding corn.

The course of the ball having a downward tendency was from the fact of his having the meal on his shoulder and in a stooping position. He managed to reach the house and went in. The Indians charged and fired many shots. The Frenchman was brave and seizing the shot gun, fired and killed an Indian. The wounded Westfall tore a board from a crack in the log structure and aimed his gun, but the Indians quickly ran away from in front of it. The Frenchman attempted to fire the other barrel of his gun through the door which had not been shut, but was hit by a ball and instantly killed. The ball struck in the breast, glanced a little on the breast bone and then went deep into his body.

He turned when hit and sat his gun against the wall in a leaning position, almost ready to fall over, and then sank down beside it and died. The gun was in this position and one barrel loaded when Wallace first entered the cabin. During this time Westfall had sunk upon the bed and thought he was dying. He was very weak and at times he was almost unconscious.

The dog, George Washington, joined in the fight, leaped the yard fence and tore all the rigging off one Indian, even the quiver from his back, but was mortally wounded and came back to the house and died close to the Frenchman. Westfall let his gun still protrude through the crack and the Indians not knowing the situation inside, went off without making another charge.

Westfall lay the balance of the day, which was from about noon, all night and part of the next day before attempting to get up. Part of that time he knew nothing at all.

Seeing he had some chance for life, Westfall got up and with great pain succeeded in getting the dead Louie out of the house by pulling at him with his left hand a little at a time. The dog was also gotten out in the same way, as he did not want them to decay in the house. Not being able to carry his gun, he hid it in some weeds. He had two horses tied in the brush, but supposing the Indians got them, did not go to look. He was not able to ride even if he had the horses.

Wallace and some others went back and buried the Frenchman and also the dog.

The horses were found nearly starved to death; the Indians failing to see them. The poor animals had eaten all the grass and bushes around them and even the grass roots in the ground.

Wallace could not find Westfall's gun; he had hid it so well and it was not found until Westfall himself was able to go get it, and then it was badly rusted. Westfall was a long time getting well, and in fact never did entirely recover from that fearful wound. It always hurt him.

Wallace brought him books and papers to read while he was lying up, and often came to see him.

One of Westfall's brothers came to Texas and lived with him some time at the ranch after getting up from his wound and they raised a good many cattle. When it was no longer frontier, however, Westfall sold out and moved down on Calaveras Creek, about fifteen miles southwest of San Antonio, and opened up a farm. Here he married, but had no family except his wife. He died in June 1897 at his home two miles from the town of Elmendorf on the Aransas Pass road. His property was valued at $5000, which he willed to his wife to be used by her until her death, at which time the money would be invested in the purchase of a free public library and reading rooms in San Antonio for both whites and blacks, but to have separate reading rooms.

CHAPTER XXVII

TAKES A TRIP BACK TO THE OLD HOME - JOHN BROWN'S RAID ON HARPER'S FERRY.

In 1859 Captain Wallace concluded he would take a trip to the old home in Virginia and go see all his kinfolk. He got up all the money he needed for an extended trip and set out. He was too sharp to carry his money in a common pocket book in his pocket, and thereby got his way with a pick pocket in New Orleans. This light-fingered gent managed to relieve him of his purse, but it makes the old man smile till yet to think what a look of disgust and disappointment must have come over his face when he examined the contents. It was full and heavy, but consisted of needles, thread, bullets and buttons.

By this time his name was famous in Texas, and his people had heard of his exploits, even in Virginia. Some of them treated him with the greatest consideration, while others, who were wealthy and aristocratic, were shocked with his rough garb and unique ways. They did not refuse to claim relationship with him, but tried to dress him up and refine him, but Bigfoot got away with them in all these things.

While stopping with one of his aunts, Elizabeth Hoffman, who was 102 years of age, John Brown made his famous raid on Harper's Ferry. Bigfoot at once began to get ready to go with some cadets who were ordered to the scene of the trouble. His aunt, however, persuaded him not to go as she was uneasy about the negroes rising. Bigfoot kept posted in regard to the latest news and would at once inform his old aunt of everything of importance that was transpiring. She would ask him every time he came in with news, if the negroes had risen yet. Wallace finally said: "No, wish they would, so that if they come fooling around here we can have black soup for dinner." The good old lady believed he meant all he said, and holding up her hands in horror, said: "William! William! What have you come to since you went to Texas?"

Captain Wallace concluded while he was on a trip that he would go over into Canada. So, after looking at the Niagara Falls, he went over, but was soon stopped by an official who said his valise would have to be examined before he went any farther.

"What do you want to examine it for?" asked Wallace.

"To see what is in it," was the reply.

"Oh, if that is all you want, I can tell you what is in it. There are two shirts, one pair of pants and a plug of tobacco."

The fellow then informed him that his son, who was the inspector, would have to look into it, but that he was at breakfast and to put down his valise and wait.

"That's a devil of a note" says Wallace "having to wait here until your son fools around and eats his breakfast. I'll not do it," and with that, went on up the hill with his valise. The man followed, yelling at him to stop, that he would be arrested, until quite a crowd collected to see what the row as about.

One red faced Irishman came through the crowd shouting "let me at him. I know what he is. He is a damned old Fenian." Wallace laid down his valise, pulled off his coat and waving his long arms at the Irishman, said: "Come here honey, I want to hug you. Whoop pa! Come into my arms. I ain't had no fun since I left Texas." The red faced fellow stopped and a tall Englishman with the longest neck Wallace says he ever saw, came up and asked him what the row was about and if he was from Texas. Wallace answered in the affirmative as to the latter, and to the other, he thought that damned Irishman wanted to fight. He then asked Wallace if he was from near San Antonio and if he knew John Twohig, banker.

"Yes," said Bigfoot, "What do you want to know about him?"

"Nothing, only I had a business transaction with him once."

Suffice it to say, things were arranged without any further damage being done and Wallace went on his way.

Not liking the looks of things on that side, however, he soon came back on the American side without taking much of a trip towards the interior.

Soon after this, Wallace said he "wouldn't give Texas for the whole shootin' match," and set out on his return to the Lone Star State, and finally arrived at his log cabin on the Chicon.

CHAPTER XXVIII

INDIAN FIGHT ON SECO.

After getting settled again on the ranch, Captain Wallace resumed his old habits of hunting, trailing Indians, and seeing about his stock; glad to once more tread his favorite haunts with dogs and gun.

In 1861, about the commencement of the Civil War between the North and South, the Comanche Indians made a most daring raid through the Sabinal and Hondo country, killing a great many people, and carrying off a large drove of horses. Runners were sent far and near to notify the settlers, and one came on a swift horse to inform Bigfoot Wallace, and ask him to take command of the men who were gathering to fight the Indians. Captain Wallace lost no time in getting to the scene, and soon between thirty and forty men were together and on the trail.

The Indians moved quick and started back to the mountains with their booty before the settlers could collect enough men to risk a battle.

The trail went out up Seco Creek and struck the mountains where the ranch of John Rheinhart now is. The men were eager to have a fight, but a great many of them were young fellows and hard to control. They would break away, half a dozen of them at once from the main body, and gallop forward or to the right or left, to look at something they thought might be an Indian. Wallace would scold and expostulate, telling them they would run their heads into a hornet's nest directly, but it did not have much effect on them.

Among the men who were in the crowd, and some of them good Indian fighters, were Judge Davenport and his young son William, John Kennedy, Ross Kennedy, Jack Davenport, Frank Hilburn, Lewis McCombs, George Robins, Lon Moore, Bill Mullins, Manuel Wydick, F. G. Finley, Nathan Davis, Malcom Van Pelt, and many others whose names cannot now be recalled. One young fellow named Harris, who lived at Ben Duncan's, was also one of the party.

At that time there was a small settlement in Sabinal Canyon and also on the Medina where Bandera is now, but there was no road connecting the two places through the mountain except a bridle path. When the party of white men struck the trail where it crossed the Seco Canyon, Captain Wallace halted the men and rode up the trail a short distance towards the Bandera side. He reported that four of the Indians had left the main body and had run someone along this trail.

It was afterwards learned that it was the tax assessor of Bandera County who was coming over to Sabinal Canyon to make assessments. The Indians killed him and got his horse, saddle and sixshooter. The Comanches had spies out watching for pursuits and seeing them coming up Seco Canyon, stopped at the head of the creek in the rough gorges to give them battle. They also tied a horse on the side of the mountain for a decoy and hid themselves nearby in the rocks and bushes. When Wallace and his party rounded the point of a mountain which stood out in the valley detached from the balance with a gully between, the horse on the side of the mountain was in plain view.

A lot of the young fellows raised a shout, crying, "My horse, my horse," and dashed up towards him. Wallace shouted to them to hold on, that it was an Indian trick, but it was of no use. On they went. Before they reached the horse, a volley from guns met them and Indians showed themselves in various places, continued to shoot and yell, and charge down among them. Bill Davenport and his horse were both wounded as was also young Harris and his horse.

Some of the men in the rear had partly ascended the hill, and the boys in front who had been fired on, ran back into the second squad. They in turn gave way and all came down on Wallace and the others. The whole business got into confusion.

In vain Wallace shouted and cursed and had to slide down a bluff himself to avoid a general rush of the Indians. Some few of the men commenced firing. Some went to the assistance of Judge Davenport who had run almost into the Indians to assist his wounded son back down the mountain. Captain Wallace was in an exposed place although he was under a ledge of rocks. The Indians were close and not being able to see him, began to hurl rocks down there, one of which struck Wallace's gun.

Judge Davenport brought his son to where Wallace was and laid him down under a cedar tree. Most of the men by this time had dismounted. Tieing their horses, they began to fight. Among these were Lewis McCombs, Lon Moore, John Kennedy, Hilburn and others. Hilburn killed one Indian and others were hit. The Indians took refuge behind the rocks so the men below could not see them, but were exposed to their fire.

John Kennedy and others who had long range guns, ascended the hill in the rear, before mentioned, and then opened fire again, shooting over the heads of the men in the gap below. Kennedy killed one Indian and they moved back from the fire. Frequently a man would break from cover and run through an exposed place and join Wallace and Davenport at the upper ledge. Among these were

Jack Davenport, Malcom Van Pelt, Nathan Davis and George Robins.

The Indians then made a charge on those coming around a point where they could see them, and several shots were exchanged. Captain Wallace knocked one Indian down with his fist and George Robins fired a load of buckshot at one not more than twenty steps distant, but he caught the charge on his shield and they rattled harmlessly to the ground. This, however, drove the Indians back and they soon after quit the fight, but they carried the horses with them. The horses were in a cedar brake in the rear of the Indians.

The tax assessor's pistol was found on the ground where the Indians had fought and also six shotguns and one hat. The guns belonged to men whom the Indians had killed on the raid. One of these was Mustang Moore who was killed on the spot where Moore's Station is on the International Road.

Young Davenport was suffering considerably from a bullet wound which was clear through the thigh.

Malcom Van Pelt asked if there was any man in the crowd who had on a linen shirt. No one showed up, but one man said he had linen wristbands on his shirt sleeves. Van Pelt said that would do. They were torn off and carefully picked to pieces and twisted into a string. This was then run through Davenport's wound and left for the time being. Someone wanted to cut the leg of the boy's pants off, but Van Pelt objected to that, as he was the doctor, saying it would freeze since it was then nearly night and had begun to sleet.

From the battleground Wallace and his men went over into Sabinal Canyon to the Ware Settlement, where they could get treatment for the wounded. The wound of Harris was not severe.

The next day Wallace took his men and some new recruits and went after the Indians again. His idea was to get ahead of them and lay an ambush. This was well executed by travelling up Sabinal Canyon, which could be done more rapidly than the Indians could cross the mountains and gorges with stolen horses.

Wallace knew the whole country and where they would strike the divide. It was not far from the Frio Water Hole, where he and Westfall had fought the Lipans in 1848.

As soon as Wallace was satisfied the Indians had not passed, he placed his men in secure ambush directly in their path. If all had obeyed orders, they would have given them a total defeat.

The force of Indians was supposed to be about equal to the whites, but some who were along think there were seventy-five of them. Wallace gave instructions for no man to fire until the Indians were in short range of their ambush. They were heard coming long before any of them came in view. The horses made a great deal of noise coming over the rocks.

The first Indians to come in sight were two riding abreast, two hundred yards away. At sight of them, Hilburn raised his gun and fired, and spoiled the whole thing. The Indians scattered everywhere and although pursued, none of them were killed. Captain Wallace ran one some distance and saw him throw something away that looked like a pair of saddle bags and about as large. Not being able to catch the Indian, he turned to see what he had lost. It proved to be two big chunks of beef tied together with horse hair. This was secured and eaten that night for supper.

The horses were collected, nearly two hundred in number, and carried back to the settlement. Hilburn said his gun went off accidentally.

CHAPTER XXIX

THE CIVIL WAR - GOING TO MEXICO AFTER COFFEE.

During the civil war Captain Wallace remained on the frontier to help protect it and see to the women and children whose husbands and fathers were in the army. Provisions could be had easy enough, but the great cry was for coffee. They tried everything for a substitute such as parched potatoes, peas, okra, meal, bran, etc. Nothing, however, would answer and whenever Wallace went among the people to see if they needed help, all their cry was for coffee. Finally he told them if they would quit making so much fuss about it, he would go to Mexico and bring them a mule load of coffee. Wallace made his word good, riding one mule and leading another across the Rio Grande to the nearest Mexican town. There were plenty of Texans across there who Wallace knew. Among others there was Licurigas Ward who helped Wallace get the coffee, and he came back with his mule loaded. They had a fine time among the women when Wallace went about over the settlements and divided the coffee. Wallace says the women would sit up all night, parch and make coffee, and drink and talk. It did him good to see them enjoy it.

When the country began to settle up around Captain Wallace, there was one Methodist preacher named Irvin Jones who was a tolerable near neighbor. He complained, among others, of the depredations of the lobos among their stock catching nearly all of their calves.

Wallace concluded he would try and kill them out. He first killed a deer, cut some of it up into small pieces, put poison in it and dragged the balance far into the night, distributing his small pieces every half mile. He finally stopped upon the creek to spend the balance of the night and then take the backtrack and see how many he had killed.

There was a large drift near where Wallace had laid down to sleep. The coons kept such a racket in the drift, that he could not sleep and finally he got up, procured a pole and yelled and beat on the drift until the coons ran out. Three of them went up one tree and remained there. At daylight Wallace shot a large owl and then the three coons. On the backtrack where he had dropped his baits, Wallace found nine dead lobos, about all there was in that neighborhood. Going over to the preacher's house, he said: "Brother Jones, you need not be uneasy about your calves anymore for awhile," and then told him of his successful raid. Rev. Jones was well pleased at this and told the captain whenever he wanted a bushel of potatoes, to come over and get them.

Rev. Irvin Jones now lives in Sabinal Canyon above Utopia.

Not much remains to be told of the eventful career of Bigfoot Wallace.

Speaking about eating things, Wallace says he has eaten a little of nearly everything. Mule meat in the mountains of Mexico, prairie dogs on the plains of Texas, polecat in a Mexican restaurant, and a piece of Comanche in a Lipan camp. The latter he says was the worse he ever had and did not know what it was at the time. He came into a Lipan camp when they were friendly and asked a squaw for something to eat. She ran her hand into a sack and pulling out a round looking piece of meat, handed it to him. Wallace thought it was buffalo meat and at once commenced on it, but it was tough and sweet. He soon found out it was not what he thought it was but concluded to finish it anyhow. When he got through, the old squaw looked at him and asked "Comanche good?" Wallace now realized what he had eaten, and told her no, that if he had known what she was giving him would not have taken it, that he was not aware he was eating a Comanche, but now that he had got him down, would try to keep him down. The old Indian then gave him a piece of buffalo meat.

In the Mexican war during the seige of Monterrey, the Texas troops forced the upper part of the city and fought their way to the Hidalgo Hotel, and there made a halt. The Mexicans had all left except the cooks and they were nearly scared to death. The men, however, told them that they had nothing to fear, as they wanted some cooks about that time of day. The men were terribly hungry but there was nothing to cook. Everything had been removed. Some sheep, however, were soon found in an enclosure and thirteen of them were killed and skinned. The cooks were then put to work and soon had the meat cooking nicely, but there was no bread to eat with it.

A dried up looking man who did not seem to think anyone would hurt him, was hanging around, and said if they would give him a dollar, he would bring them a blanket full of bread. Wallace handed him a dollar and told him to skin out quick and get it. The Mexican was good at his word and soon came back with as much bread as he could carry in his blanket.

One of the men said he was afraid to eat the bread, that it might be poisoned. Wallace said he would soon see whether it was or not. Going through the bread, he picked out a loaf that looked cracked and scaly, called up the Mexican and told him to sit down there and eat it. He demurred at this, but the big Texan pulled his pistol, cocked it, and the Mexican went to work on the bread. The bread was tough, but he finally worked it all down. Wallace then selected another loaf and told him to try that one.

The Mexican walled his eyes and made signs that he was choking to death. A quart of water was handed him to wash down with, and when that was all swallowed, the bread was placed in his hands. He took it and went to work on it quick but soon choked. Wallace handed him more water and encouraged him to proceed by pointing his pistol at his right eye.

This loaf was finished. The Mexican looked glad and even smiled at the little pleasant joke of Bigfoot. His countenance changed, however, when Wallace handed him another and motioned him to proceed.

Before taking the bread, the Mexican made a cross, and called on the saints. When he choked Wallace gave him more water, and he would look in despair towards the muzzle of the pistol. When the third loaf was eaten, he was told to sit down and see if it would kill him. As he did not show any signs of toppling over in two minutes, and as the mutton was cooking and steaming hot before them, the Texans concluded to risk it and pitched in.

While this dinner was being eaten which was not on the bill of fare of the Hidalgo Hotel that day, the cannons were booming. There was cheering in the lower part of town where General Taylor was carrying one street after another towards the center.

The little Mexican sat and rubbed his stomach while the hungry men were eating, and said: "Yo sentir yo comer no mas por semano." (I could eat

no more in a week.) When told he could go, there was no grass grew under his feet.

Captain Wallace is now in his eighty-second year. He is very nervous, so much so that he cannot wait upon himself at the table. He has not lived alone for ten years. Part of this time has been spent with Mr. Bramlett and Mr. Thomas. His prominent home now is with Mr. W. W. Cochran and family who live in Frio County five miles from Devine, south, and three miles north of Big Foot post office. He is a typical old Texan, free hearted, and has a good temper for a man who has passed through as much as he has.

THE END

APPENDIX

Letter written by Big Foot Wallace in which he relates some of his experiences as a prisoner in Mexico. He has also sketched a diagram of the prison at Salado, Mexico where the Black Bean episode took place.

Big foot Oct 13/88

Miss N C Franklin
San Marcos

Madam
you wished to know
if Ft Salado is still
there and it is and will
be as long as time lasts
all four are there the
water is supplied for
stock and soldiers the
wells varying from 400
to over 800 feet in
depth water drawn up
by mules by a band
running around a wheel
14 ft high that throws the water
in the cistern holding about
800 gallon barrels the
appearance of the country
is grey looking. Sandy
now and then bunch grass

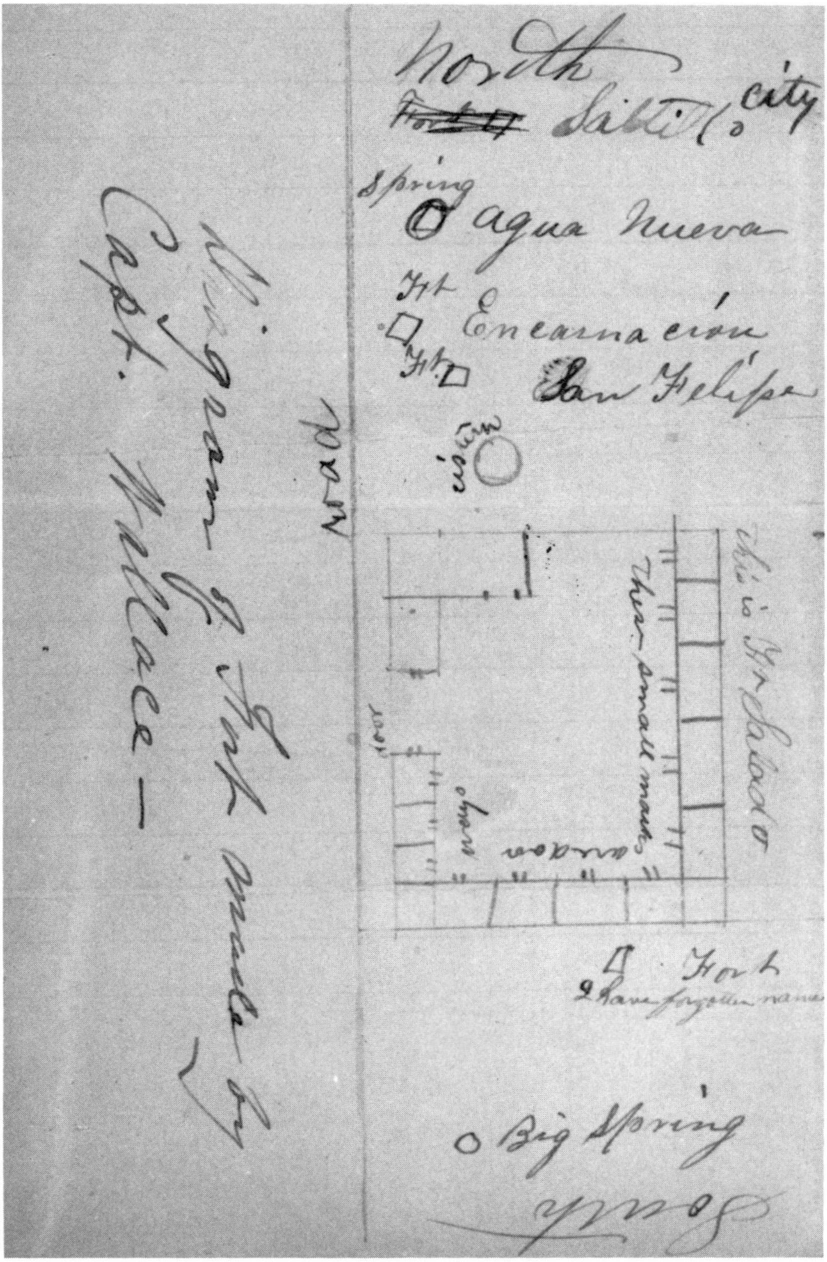

North

Saltillo city

Spring

agua Nueva

Ft

Encarnación

Ft

San Felipe

This is Ft Salado

These small marks

Fort

I have forgotten name

Big Spring

South

Diagram of Fort made by Capt. Wallace —

sage bush, range of mountains on East & West side of road of this sandy plain about 30 miles in width perfectly level at Big Spring. East range of Mountains runs out on West side is main Rocky Mountains, at the Forts there is a few Jacks and Jennets and few horses is the only stock I seen, on the dividing ridges there is scattering pine trees. you wanted to know about birds I never seen a bird nor no game of any description, next is Big Spring is a big horse ranch about 20,000 head very large Spring gushes out at the end of a mountain runs about 40 or 50 yds and forms a lake about 200 yds long.

the soil there changes al-
together of a mulatto color,
from Big Spring the col. told
us if we could make two days
travel in one day we could
lay up at a little town
called Vanau Deer town in
English there we found plenty
of fruit that evening and
next day we feasted that was
the only place on the road
that we did feast. we reached
San Louis in about 3 days travel
I lost the use of my arm
pulling my companion along who
was sick and when we arrived
there was three ladies come
to see the prisoners one of
them was the Governors wife.
the governor of San Louis Btosi
they went back and brought the Governor and a
black Smith and cut the irons
off of my arm and McMahons
arm God bless the Governor

4

wife for she saved my
life for I dont I could
have been saved in three
days longer she bought
4 bottles of Catalan and
gave them to me to rub
my arm I saw a cotton
tree in our Prison yard
they said was seven years
old and would make
a good Shade it was
about one foot through
I will quit I will give
you the balance to the
city of Mexico in my
next if you want
any more information
write I will be pleased
to give it to you

Respectfully
W A A Wallace

INDEX

INDEX

INDEX

INDEX

BOOKS OF RELATED INTEREST . . .

CAPTAIN BILL McDONALD TEXAS RANGER
BY ALBERT BIGELOW PAINE

The compelling story of one of the most famous Texas Rangers of them all. "One Riot, one Ranger" Captain Bill McDonald's daring six-gun adventures are all part of Paine's dramatic biography. Originally published in 1909. $12.95 paperback, $50.00 limited edition.

FAMOUS TEXAS FEUDS
BY C. L. DOUGLAS

The blood-stained story of the most important of the violent feuds in 19th century Texas: Regulators and Moderators, Taylor-Sutton Controversy, Elizario Salt War, Horrell-Higgins Affair, Mason County War and Jaybirds versus Woodpeckers. Originally published in 1936. $19.95 cloth, $12.95 paperback, $50.00 limited edition.

EARLY SETTLERS AND INDIAN FIGHTERS OF SOUTHWEST TEXAS
BY A. J. SOWELL

"Sketch after sketch (132 sketches in 844 pages) of men (and women) who lived and died on the frontier of Texas. Entertainingly written with the liberal use of humorous anecdotes."—American West. Originally published in 1900. $34.95 cloth, $75.00 limited edition.

Order from your favorite bookstore or from:

STATE HOUSE PRESS
Box 15247 NE Station
Austin, Texas 78761